AN 01-20ENA-1

B-47 STRATOJET
PILOT'S FLIGHT OPERATING INSTRUCTIONS

by United States Air Force

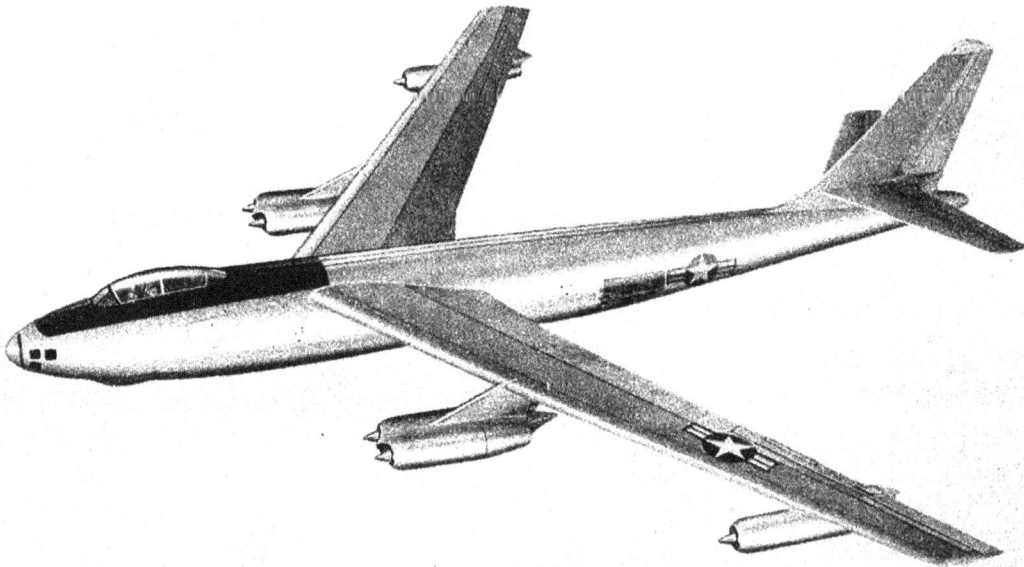

**LATEST REVISED PAGES SUPERSEDE
THE SAME PAGES OF PREVIOUS DATE**

Insert revised pages into basic
publication. Destroy superseded pages.

REVISION NOTICE

SMAMA—DEC 50—1 020

048001 A

1 JULY 1950
REVISED 30 OCTOBER 1950

Reproduction for non-military use of the information or illustrations contained in this publication is not permitted without specific approval of the issuing service (BuAer or AMC). The policy for use of Classified Publications is established for the Air Force in AFR 205-1 and for the Navy in Navy Regulations, Article 1509.

LIST OF REVISED PAGES ISSUED

INSERT LATEST REVISED PAGES. DESTROY SUPERSEDED PAGES.

NOTE: The portion of the text affected by the current revision is indicated by a vertical line in the outer margins of the page.

Page No.	Date of Latest Revision	Page No.	Date of Latest Revision	Page No.	Date of Latest Revision
* 1	30 October 1950	* 41	30 October 1950		
* ii	30 October 1950	* 42	30 October 1950		
* iii	30 October 1950	* 43	30 October 1950		
* iv	30 October 1950	* 44	30 October 1950		
* 1	30 October 1950	* 45	30 October 1950		
* 2	30 October 1950	* 47	30 October 1950		
* 3	30 October 1950	* 49	30 October 1950		
* 4	30 October 1950	* 50	30 October 1950		
* 5	30 October 1950	* 50A	30 October 1950		
* 6	30 October 1950	* 51	30 October 1950		
* 7	30 October 1950	* 52	30 October 1950		
* 8	30 October 1950	* 53	30 October 1950		
* 10	30 October 1950	* 54	30 October 1950		
* 11	30 October 1950	* 56	30 October 1950		
* 12	30 October 1950	* 57	30 October 1950		
* 13	30 October 1950	* 58	30 October 1950		
* 15	30 October 1950	* 58A	30 October 1950		
* 16	30 October 1950	* 59	30 October 1950		
* 17	30 October 1950	* 60	30 October 1950		
* 18	30 October 1950	* 62	30 October 1950		
* 20	30 October 1950	* 64	30 October 1950		
* 21	30 October 1950	* 65	30 October 1950		
* 22	30 October 1950	* 67	30 October 1950		
* 23	30 October 1950	* 68	30 October 1950		
* 24	30 October 1950	* 70	30 October 1950		
* 24A	30 October 1950	* 73	30 October 1950		
* 24B	30 October 1950	* 74	30 October 1950		
* 25	30 October 1950	* 75	30 October 1950		
* 26	30 October 1950	* 76	30 October 1950		
* 27	30 October 1950	* 77	30 October 1950		
* 28	30 October 1950	* 78	30 October 1950		
* 29	30 October 1950				
* 30	30 October 1950				
* 31	30 October 1950				
* 32	30 October 1950				

THIS MANUAL IS SOLD FOR HISTORIC RESEARCH PURPOSES ONLY, AS AN ENTERTAINMENT. IT IS NOT INTENDED TO BE USED AS PART OF AN ACTUAL FLIGHT TRAINING PROGRAM. NO BOOK CAN SUBSTITUTE FOR FLIGHT TRAINING BY AN AUTHORIZED INSTRUCTOR. THE LICENSING OF PILOTS IS OVERSEEN BY ORGANIZATIONS AND AUTHORITIES SUCH AS THE FAA AND CAA. OPERATING AN AIRCRAFT WITHOUT THE PROPER LICENSE IS A FEDERAL CRIME.

*The asterisk indicates pages revised, added or deleted by the current revision.

049002A

ADDITIONAL COPIES OF THIS PUBLICATION MAY BE OBTAINED AS FOLLOWS:

USAF

USAF ACTIVITIES.—In accordance with Technical Order No. 00-5-2
NAVY ACTIVITIES.—Submit request to nearest supply point listed below, using form Nav Aer-140: NAS, Alameda, Calif.; ASD, Orote, Guam; NAS, Jacksonville, Fla.; NAS, Norfolk, Va.; NASD, Oahu; NASD, Philadelphia, Pa.; NAS, San Diego, Calif.; NAS, Seattle, Wash.
For listing of available material and details of distribution see Naval Aeronautics Publications Index Nav Aer 00-500

TABLE OF CONTENTS

948003 A

ILLUSTRATIONS

048004 A

INTRODUCTION

SECTION I DESCRIPTION

The function of this section is to describe the airplane, its equipment, systems, and controls which are essential to flight and which will be needed for one complete noncombat mission in good weather at medium altitude. All emergency equipment which is not part of the auxiliary equipment and all miscellaneous equipment is also covered in this section.

SECTION II NORMAL OPERATING INSTRUCTIONS

This section contains the steps of procedure to be accomplished from the time the airplane is approached by the flight crew until it is left parked on the ramp after accomplishing one complete noncombat mission in good weather at medium altitude.

SECTION III EMERGENCY OPERATING INSTRUCTIONS

This section clearly and concisely describes the procedure to be followed in meeting any emergency (except those in connection with the auxiliary equipment) that could reasonably be expected to be encountered.

SECTION IV OPERATIONAL EQUIPMENT

This section includes the description, normal operation and emergency operation of all equipment not directly contributing to flight but which enables the the airplane to perform certain specialized functions. Included in this category are such items of equipment as: heating, ventilation, and pressurization systems; anti-icing system; communication equipment; lighting equipment; oxygen system; navigation equipment; bombing equipment; photographic equipment; and gunnery equipment.

APPENDIX I OPERATING DATA

This section contains the necessary charts and graphs for airspeed correction, the instrument dial markings, and graphs for making thrust calculations for take-off.

048076 A

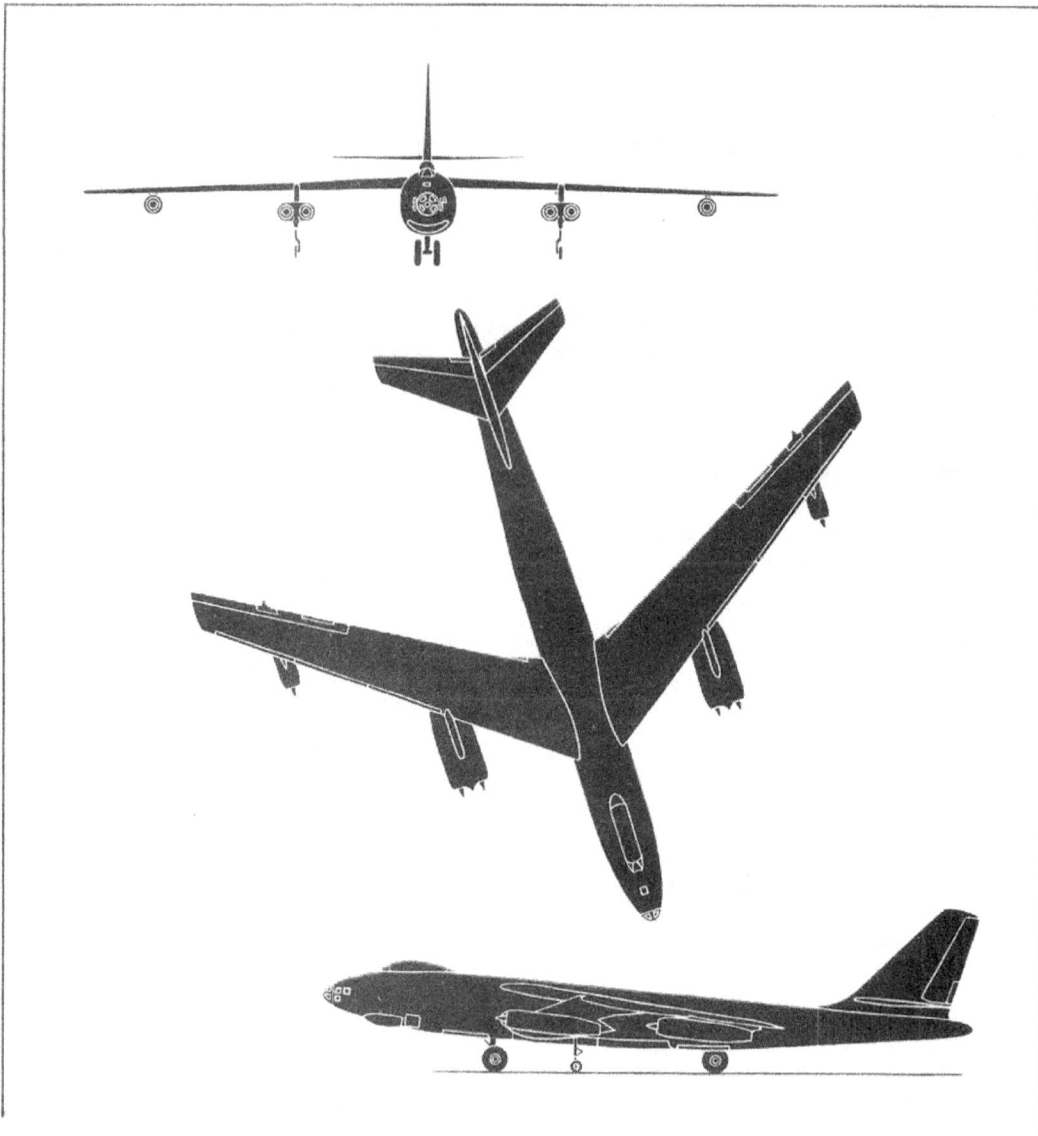

The Airplane

04B005A

SECTION ▌ DESCRIPTION

1-1. AIRPLANE.

1-2. GENERAL.

1-2A. The Boeing B-47A "Stratojet" airplane is a land based, six-engine, jet propelled, medium bomber capable of long range flight at high speeds and high altitudes. The tactical mission of the airplane is the destruction, by bombs, of land or naval material objectives. The normal crew comprises a pilot, copilot, and navigator. The additional duty of gunner is assigned to the copilot while the navigator has the additional duties of bombardier and radar operator.

1-3. OVERALL DIMENSIONS.

Wing Span . . . . 116 feet
Fuselage Length . . . . 106 feet, 9 inches
Height (to top of fin) . . . . 27 feet, 11 inches

1-4. GROSS WEIGHT. The approximate design gross weight of the airplane is 125,000 pounds.

1-5. SPECIAL FEATURES. The airplane is characterized by swept wings and empennage, underslung nacelles, and by its extremely clean appearance throughout. Innovations incorporated include a bicycle type main landing gear and internally mounted assisted take-off units. Space and structural provisions have been made to accommodate a bomb rack and general purpose bombs up to the 22,000 pound size. Provision has also been made on some airplanes to incorporate a tail turret mounting two, type M-3, caliber .50 machine guns.

1-6. INTERIOR ARRANGEMENT. All normal crew duties are accomplished in the pressurized compartment which extends from a pressure bulkhead aft of the copilot's station, forward to the nose. The pilot and copilot are provided tandem stations under the bubble canopy in the cockpit. The copilot's seat can be swiveled so that the copilot may face aft for his gunnery duties. The navigator is provided a station in the nose of the airplane which includes his navigation, bombing, and radar equipment. A walkway is provided on the left side of the fuselage from the navigator's station aft to the pressure bulkhead. Connecting to this walkway through a pressure door is the main entrance passage located in the lower left side of the fuselage. A crawlway on the left side of the forward wheel well provides access to the bomb bay area. A platform in the bomb bay is the most aft point of access in the airplane during flight.

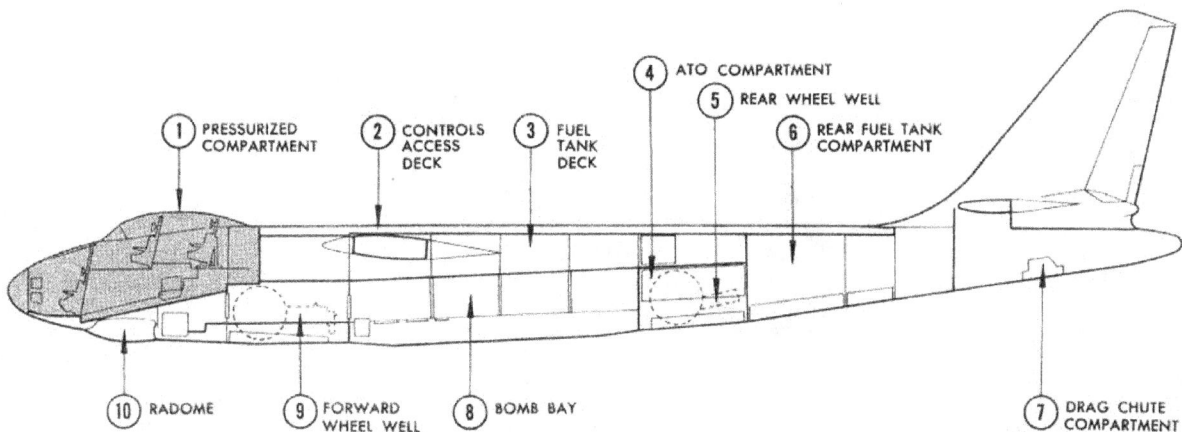

Figure 1-1. Compartments

RESTRICTED
AN 01-20ENA-1

LEGEND

1. RADAR INDICATOR
2. NAVIGATOR'S INSTRUMENT PANEL
3. BOMBARDIER'S PANEL
4. PILOT'S INSTRUMENT PANEL
5. PILOT'S SEAT
6. COPILOT'S INSTRUMENT PANEL
7. COPILOT'S SEAT
7A. CANOPY LOCK STOWAGE
8. BOMB BAY WALKWAYS
9. BOMB BAY ACCESS DOOR
10. BOMB BAY PLATFORM
11. CRAWLWAY
12. LADDER
13. ENTRANCE DOOR
14. PRESSURIZED COMPARTMENT DOOR (OPEN)
15. CREW RELIEF CONTAINERS
16. WALKWAY
17. NAVIGATOR'S SEAT
18. BOMBSIGHT STABILIZER

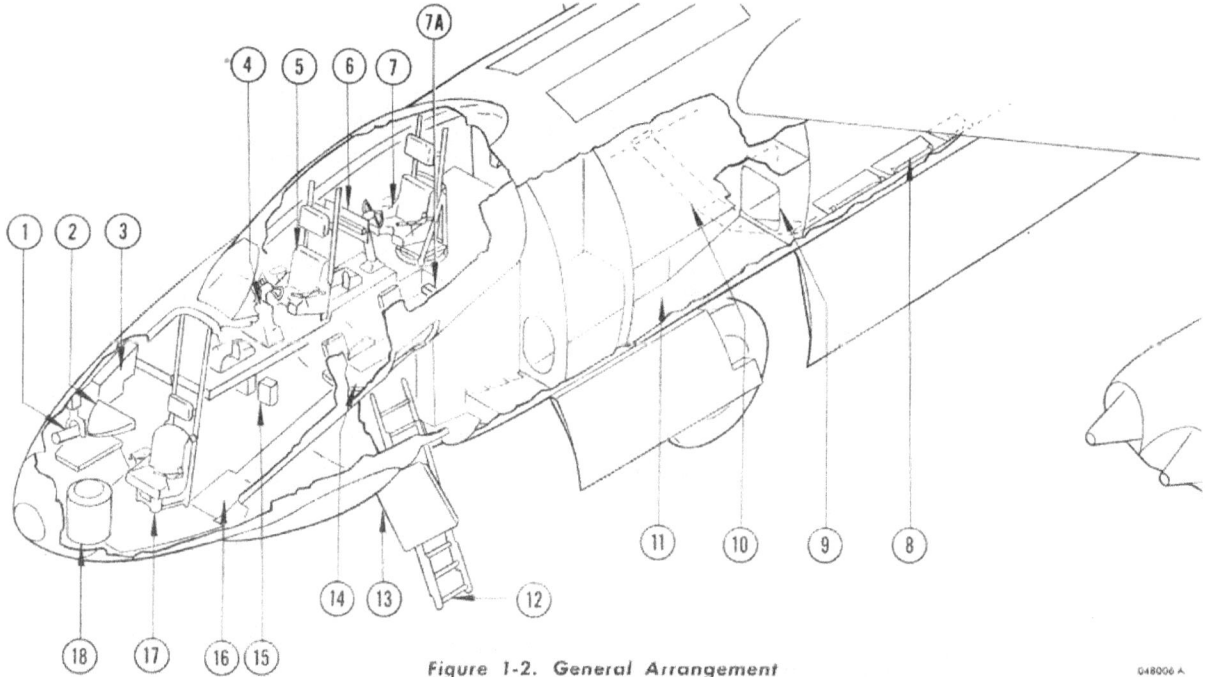

Figure 1-2. General Arrangement

048006 A

③ COPILOT'S GUNNERY STATION
② COPILOT'S NORMAL STATION
① NAVIGATOR'S STATION

④ BOMB BAY

ROUTE OF
MOVEMENT TO
BOMB BAY

COPILOT'S SEAT SWIVELS
TO COPILOT'S
GUNNERY STATION

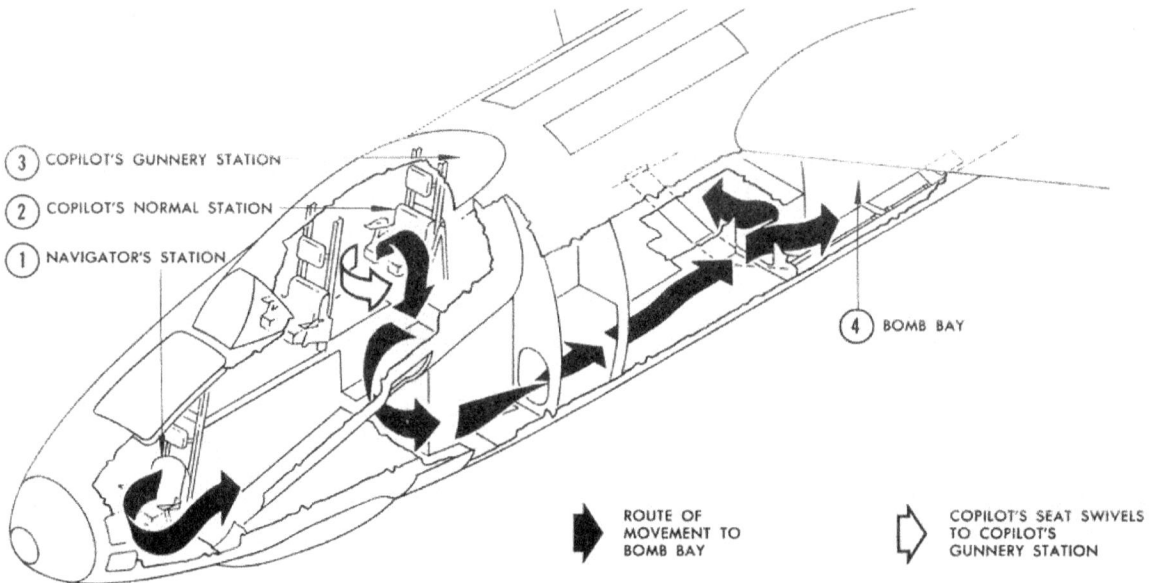

Figure 1-3. Crew Movement

048031A

RESTRICTED

Revised 30 October 1950

NOTE

A 2 TO 3% REDUCTION IN RANGE CAN RESULT
FROM SCUFFING OF THE WING SURFACES WHEN
USING THEM AS A WALKWAY; ALL PERSONNEL
MUST BE EXTREMELY CAREFUL TO RETAIN THE
AERODYNAMIC CLEANNESS OF THE AIRPLANE
DURING SERVICING OPERATIONS.

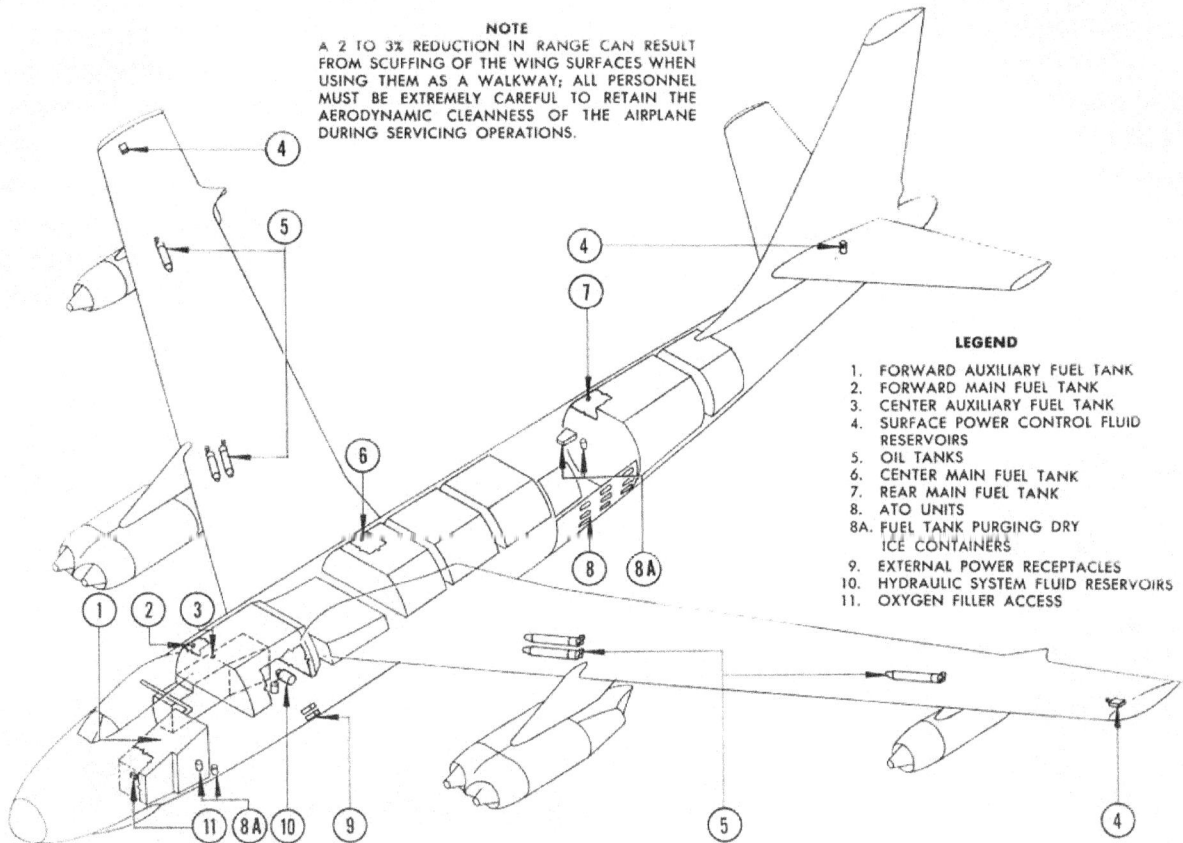

LEGEND

1. FORWARD AUXILIARY FUEL TANK
2. FORWARD MAIN FUEL TANK
3. CENTER AUXILIARY FUEL TANK
4. SURFACE POWER CONTROL FLUID
   RESERVOIRS
5. OIL TANKS
6. CENTER MAIN FUEL TANK
7. REAR MAIN FUEL TANK
8. ATO UNITS
8A. FUEL TANK PURGING DRY
   ICE CONTAINERS
9. EXTERNAL POWER RECEPTACLES
10. HYDRAULIC SYSTEM FLUID RESERVOIRS
11. OXYGEN FILLER ACCESS

Figure 1-4. Servicing

048007 A

1-7. ENGINE.

1-8. GENERAL.

1-9. The airplane is powered by six J47-GE-11 axial flow, turbo-jet engines. A single engine is mounted in each outboard nacelle and two parallel engines in each inboard nacelle. When viewed in the direction of flight, the engines are numbered from left to right with the left outboard engine being number one. The conventional jet engine controls and accessories are provided. In addition, on some airplanes, electrically operated nacelle close-off doors are provided in each engine air inlet for use during engine failures or fires.

1-10. CONTROLS.

1-11. THROTTLES. The pilot's throttles comprise a master throttle (5, figure 1-6) and six individual throttles (4, figure 1-6). The copilot is provided with only a master throttle (6, figure 1-15) which is cable connected to the pilot's master throttle. All throttle quadrants are marked "CUTOFF" at the aft end of travel, "IDLE" at the approximate idling position, and "OPEN" at the forward end of travel. Prior to forward motion, the individual throttles are

locked in the "CUTOFF" position until released by the throttle knobs being lifted. During aft motion, the individual throttles cannot be retarded below the approximately 35% RPM position until released by the throttle knobs. The throttles cannot be advanced beyond approximately the 52% RPM position when the surface lock lever (6, figure 1-6) is in the "LOCK" position. The master throttles will move all six individual throttles providing the individual throttles are unlocked. The principle function of the throttles is to adjust the fuel regulators to maintain the desired RPM. In addition, the fuel, oil, hydraulic, warning, and ignition systems are partially controlled by microswitches which are actuated by the throttles.

1-12. All throttle microswitches are automatically actuated by throttle motion. The fuel tank valve and fuel fire shutoff valve are closed and the fuel boost pump turned off for an engine when its individual throttle is placed in the "CUTOFF" position. The oil and hydraulic fire shutoff valves for an engine are closed only when its individual throttle is placed in "CUTOFF" and the fire button (11, figure 1-8) is actuated. The fuel tank valve is opened, the boost pump energized, the fuel fire shutoff valve opened, the oil and hydraulic fire shutoff valves opened (if previously closed), and the ignition transformers energized for an engine when its individual throttle is advanced to the "IDLE" position. The landing gear warning switches are actuated by the individual throttles and the flap warning switch is actuated by the master throttle.

1-13. THROTTLE LOCK LEVER. The throttles are prevented from creeping by a "LOCKED--UN-LOCKED" throttle lock lever (18, figure 1-6) on the pilot's control stand. When the lever is in the aft, or "UNLOCKED" position, the throttles are free to move. When the lever is advanced, increasing amounts of friction are applied to the master throttle

directly, and to the individual throttles through master throttle linkage.

1-14. IGNITION SWITCHES. Six "NORMAL--OFF-- ALTITUDE START AND TEST" ignition switches (7, figure 1-6) are on the ignition switch panel. When the switches are in the "OFF" position, the ignition transformers and spark plugs are not energized. When the switches have been actuated to the "NOR-MAL" position, the ignition circuits are armed so that ignition will occur as soon as the starter switches (11, figure 1-11) have been actuated to "START" and the throttles have been advanced to, or beyond the "IDLE" position. "NORMAL" ignition termi-

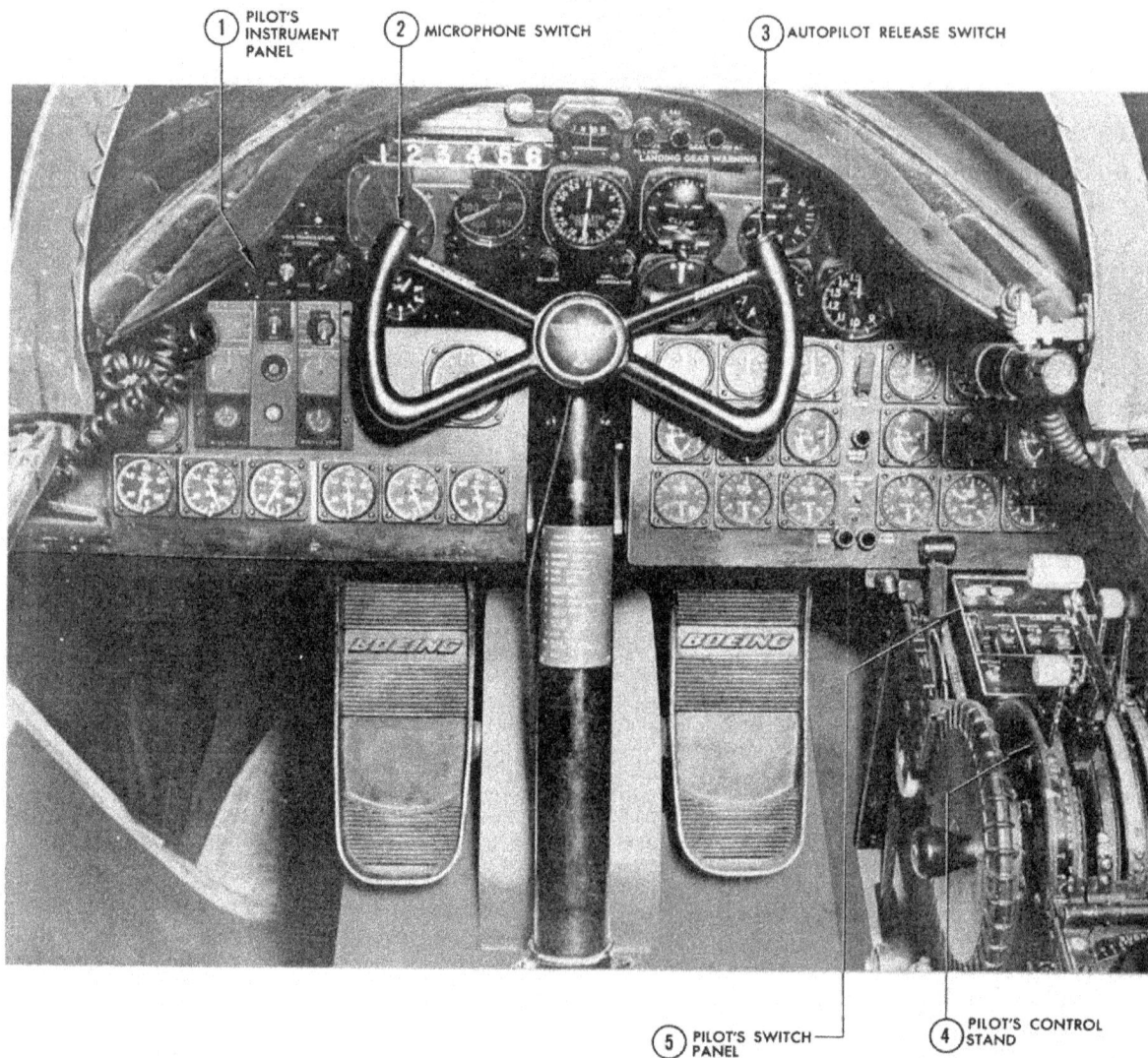

Figure 1-5. Pilot's Station

LEGEND

1. STEERING RATIO SELECTOR LEVER	12. SURFACE POWER CONTROL PANEL
2. PILOT'S SWITCH PANEL	13. LANDING GEAR EMERGENCY RETRACTION SWITCH
2A. DRAG CHUTE DEPLOYMENT HANDLE	14. LANDING GEAR CONTROL LEVER
3. FIRE WARNING TEST PANEL	15. AILERON TRIM CONTROL KNOB AND INDICATOR
4. INDIVIDUAL THROTTLES	16. RUDDER PEDAL ADJUSTMENT KNOB
5. MASTER THROTTLE	16A. DRAG CHUTE JETTISON HANDLE
6. SURFACE LOCK LEVER	17. ELEVATOR TRIM CONTROL KNOB AND INDICATOR
7. IGNITION SWITCHES	18. THROTTLE LOCK LEVER
8. RUDDER TRIM CONTROL KNOB AND INDICATOR	19. PILOT'S CONTROL STAND
9. WING FLAP LEVER	20. LANDING GEAR WARNING HORN RELEASE LEVER
10. FUEL CONTROL PANEL	21. HEAT SELECTOR KNOB
10A. CANOPY LOCK LEVER	
11. PILOT'S RADIO CONTROL PANEL	

Figure 1-6. Pilot's Station—Right Side

04B032A

nates automatically when either automatic or manual cutoff of the starter occurs. When the ignition switches are actuated to the "ALTITUDE START AND TEST" position, the spark plugs are energized continuously regardless of the starter switch and throttle positions. The use of this position is limited to 3 minutes during ground operations.

1-15. STARTER SWITCHES. Six "START--OFF-- CUTOFF" starter switches (11, figure 1-11) are on the pilot's switch panel. When the switches are in the "OFF" position, circuits are closed which allow the starter-generators to be used as generators. When in "START" or "CUTOFF," the switches are spring-loaded to "OFF." When the switches are actuated to the "START" position, the starter-generators are motorized for starting, the ignition circuits are armed, and (on engines 3 and 4 only) the hydraulic pump pressure release valves are opened. When the switches return to the "OFF" positions, the starter-generators remain motorized for starting until an automatic cutoff device shifts them to be used as generators. When external power is disconnected, the "CUTOFF" position provides a manual means of accomplishing cutoff of a starter in the event of automatic cutoff failure. Circuit breakers for the starter control circuit are on the copilot's circuit breaker panel (3, figure 1-24).

1-16. FIRE BUTTON. A push-button switch (11, figure 1-18) on the pilot's instrument panel, when depressed, will close circuits to actuate the oil and hydraulic fire shutoff valves on any engine for which the individual throttle has been retarded to "CUT-OFF." When the button is released, the valves will remain closed until the throttle has been advanced to the "IDLE" position. The alternator fields on the engine No. 1 or No. 6 alternators will be de-energized when the No. 1 or No. 6 throttle is retarded to "CUTOFF" and the fire button is depressed. Also, the generator fields

on each engine will be deenergized in the same manner.

1-17. NACELLE CLOSE-OFF DOOR BUTTON. On some airplanes, nacelle close-off doors are provided at each engine air inlet. These doors are electrically operated by placing the desired throttle to "CUTOFF" and actuating a push-button nacelle close-off door switch on the pilot's instrument panel. The doors are automatically reopened when the throttle is returned to the "IDLE" position. Circuit breakers for the system are on the main AC power shield and copilot's circuit breaker panel (1, and 3, figure 1-24).

1-18. INDICATORS.

1-19. TACHOMETERS. Engine speed in per cent of RPM is indicated by 12 tachometers, 6 of which are on the pilot's instrument panel (31, figure 1-8) and 6 on the copilot's instrument panel (4, figure 1-18).

1-20. EXHAUST TEMPERATURE INDICATORS. The temperature of the exhaust gases in degrees centigrade is indicated by six exhaust temperature indicators (28, figure 1-8) on the pilot's instrument panel.

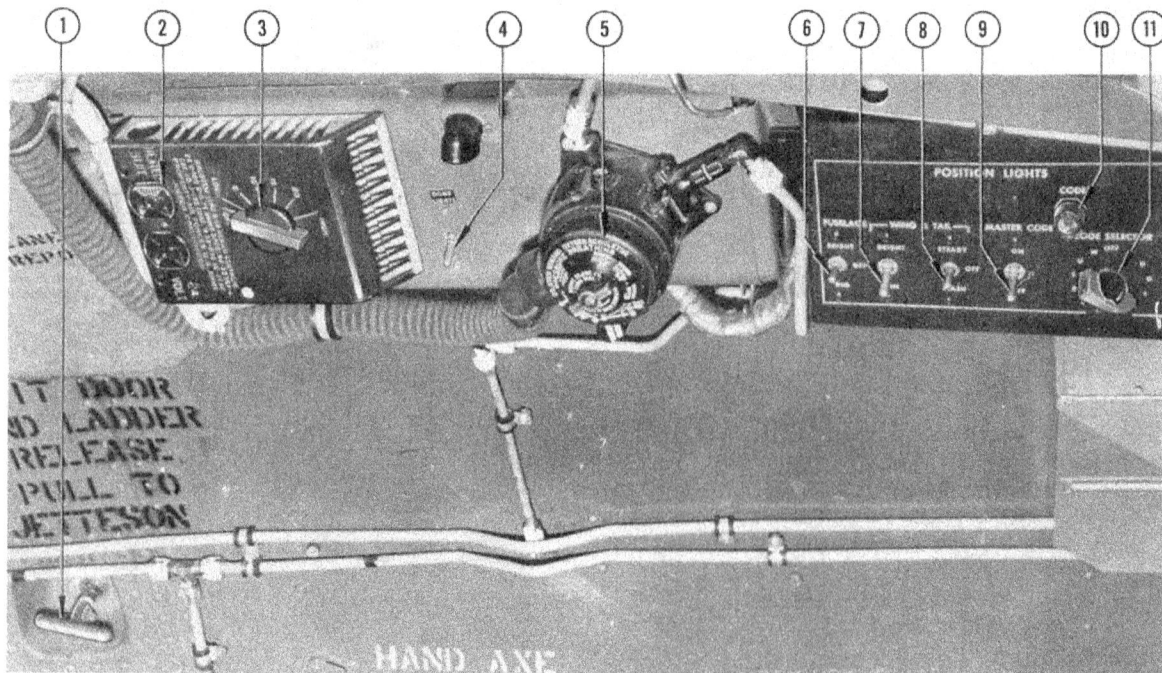

LEGEND

1. EMERGENCY DOOR AND LADDER RELEASE HANDLE
2. SUIT HEATER RECEPTACLES
3. SUIT HEATER RHEOSTAT
4. WALKWAY DOME AND ENTRANCE LIGHTS SWITCH
5. OXYGEN REGULATOR
6. FUSELAGE POSITION LIGHTS SWITCH
7. WING AND TAIL POSITION LIGHTS DIMMING SWITCH
8. WING AND TAIL POSITION LIGHTS SWITCH
9. MASTER CODE SWITCH
10. MASTER CODE INDICATING LIGHT
11. CODE SELECTOR KNOB

Figure 1-7. Pilot's Station—Left Side

1-21. OIL SYSTEM.

1-22. GENERAL.

1-22A. On this airplane, each engine is provided an independent oil system including an oil tank and two engine-driven oil pumps. Each tank holds 10 U.S. gallons and has an expansion space of 2 U.S. gallons. A combination pressure and scavenge pump supplies clean oil at the proper lubricating temperature through jet nozzles to all bearings and to the accessory section gears. In addition, a scavenge pump is provided to return the oil from the rotor bearing sump to the oil tank. The oil pressure pump also supplies oil to a fuel control regulator from which variable control oil is metered to a fuel pressure regulator. The oil tanks are pressurized by air bled from the wing anti-icing ducts to prevent foaming. Cooling of the return

oil is accomplished automatically by transferring the heat from the oil to the fuel flowing into the combustion chambers.

This transfer is accomplished by the use of a heat exchanger between the return oil line and the fuel line.

1-23. OIL SPECIFICATION AND GRADE. The oil used in this airplane shall conform to Specification AF No. 3519, amendment 1, Grade 1005 (summer and winter).

1-24. CONTROLS.

1-25. FIRE BUTTON. An oil system fire shutoff valve is energized to its closed position when a fire button (11, figure 1-8) on the pilot's instrument panel is pressed and the throttle for the malfunctioning

LEGEND

1. CABIN ALTIMETER
2. OXYGEN PRESSURE GAGE
3. OXYGEN FLOW INDICATOR
4. AUTOPILOT CONTROL PANEL
5. DIRECTIONAL DAMPER SWITCH
6. HEAT SELECTOR SWITCH
7. CABIN TEMPERATURE SELECTOR RHEOSTAT
8. DATA INDICATOR
9. FIRE WARNING LIGHTS
10. MAXIMUM ALLOWABLE AIRSPEED INDICATOR
11. FIRE BUTTON
12. GYROSYN COMPASS
13. MAGNETIC COMPASS
14. ATTITUDE GYRO
15. LANDING GEAR WARNING LIGHTS
16. TURN-AND-BANK INDICATOR
17. RATE-OF-CLIMB INDICATOR
18. ALTIMETER
19. FLAP POSITION INDICATOR
20. MACHMETER
21. CLOCK
22. WINDSHIELD OVERHEAT CYCLING LIGHT
23. BOMB SALVO SWITCH
24. BOMBS AWAY LIGHT
25. CABIN AIR THERMOMETER
26. FREE AIR THERMOMETER
27. FUEL PRESSURE INDICATORS
28. EXHAUST TEMPERATURE INDICATORS
29. BOMB DOOR POSITION LIGHTS
30. BOMB DOOR CONTROL SWITCH
31. TACHOMETERS
32. ANTI-SKID INOPERATIVE LIGHT
33. MARKER BEACON LIGHT
34. RADIO COMPASS INDICATOR
35. ACCELEROMETER
36. OIL PRESSURE INDICATORS
37. EMERGENCY CANOPY RELEASE HANDLE
38. BRAKE LOCK KNOB

Figure 1-8. Pilot's Instrument Panel

04B034A

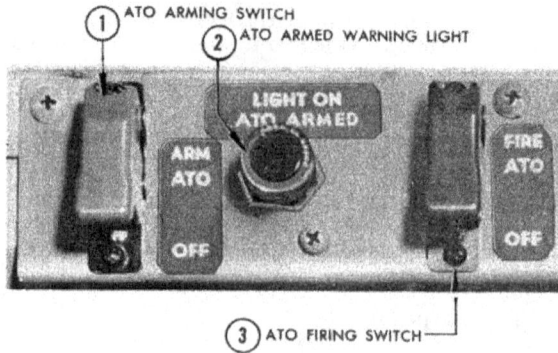

Figure 1-9. ATO Control Panel 048035A

LEGEND

1. EMERGENCY ALARM SWITCH
2. LANDING LIGHT SWITCHES
3. ANTI-SKID SWITCH
4. MASTER AIR CONDITIONING SWITCH
5. AIR SELECTOR SWITCH
6. CABIN PRESSURE SELECTOR SWITCH
7. WINDSHIELD HEAT SWITCH
8. CANOPY DEFROST SWITCH
9. PITOT HEAT SWITCHES
10. WING SLAT WARNING HORN SWITCH
11. STARTER SWITCHES
12. BATTERY SWITCH

Figure 1-11. Pilot's Switch Panel 048037 A

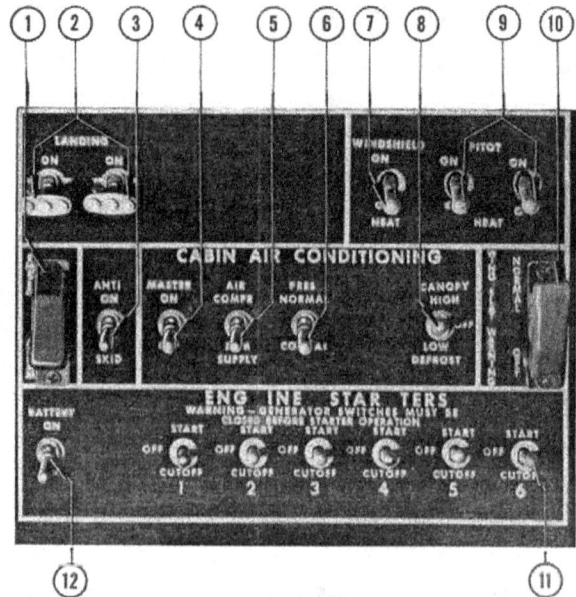

Figure 1-10. Fire Warning Test Panel 048036A

engine has been retarded to the "CUTOFF" position.
This valve is automatically energized to its open
position when the throttle is again advanced to the
"IDLE" position.

1-26. INDICATORS.

1-27. OIL PRESSURE INDICATORS. Engine oil
pressure is indicated by six oil pressure indicators
(36, figure 1-8) on the pilot's instrument panel.

1-28. FUEL SYSTEM.

1-29. GENERAL.

1-29A. The main fuel supply consists of three tanks
housed within the fuselage structure. Each tank
provides fuel for one engine on each side of the
airplane. The forward main tank provides fuel for
engines No. 1 and No. 6; the center main tank for
engines No. 2 and No. 5; and the rear main tank
for engines No. 3 and No. 4. All main tanks can

be manifolded to supply fuel from any tank to any
engine. However, check valves prevent transfer
of fuel between main tanks. Two auxiliary tanks
are provided; the forward auxiliary tank feeding
into the forward main tank and the center auxiliary tank feeding into the center main tank.
Each main tank is provided with four boost pumps,
one for each side of the airplane in the extreme
forward end and the extreme aft end of the tank.
One boost pump is provided in each auxiliary
tank. A fuel tank valve is mounted on the outlet
of each boost pump. Dry ice fuel tank purging
is provided for all tanks. Dry ice containers
continuously release CO_2 into the air space
in the fuel tanks to alleviate any potential fire
hazard.

1-30. The normal flow of fuel for each engine is
from the boost pumps, through the fuel tank valves
and check valves, to a fuel fire shutoff valve. From
the fuel fire shutoff valve fuel is delivered to the
engine-driven fuel pump which supplies the nozzles
in the combustion chambers. A by-pass around the
engine-driven fuel pump, through a fuel control
valve, controls the pressure to the nozzles. Variable control oil from a fuel regulator in the oil
system provides a governing effect on the fuel control valve. The throttle acts on the fuel regulator
to set the fuel pressure to which the engine is to be
governed.

LEGEND

1. FUEL QUANTITY INDICATOR TEST SWITCHES
2. FUEL BOOST PRESSURE WARNING LIGHTS
3. FUEL SELECTOR SWITCHES
4. FORWARD AUXILIARY FUEL TANK QUANTITY INDICATOR
5. FORWARD AUXILIARY TANK VALVE AND BOOST PUMP SWITCH
6. FORWARD AUXILIARY FUEL TANK PRESSURE INDICATOR
7. CENTER AUXILIARY FUEL TANK PRESSURE INDICATOR
8. CENTER AUXILIARY TANK VALVE AND BOOST PUMP SWITCH
9. CENTER AUXILIARY FUEL TANK QUANTITY INDICATOR
10. PANEL LIGHT RHEOSTATS
11. MAIN TANK FUEL QUANTITY INDICATORS

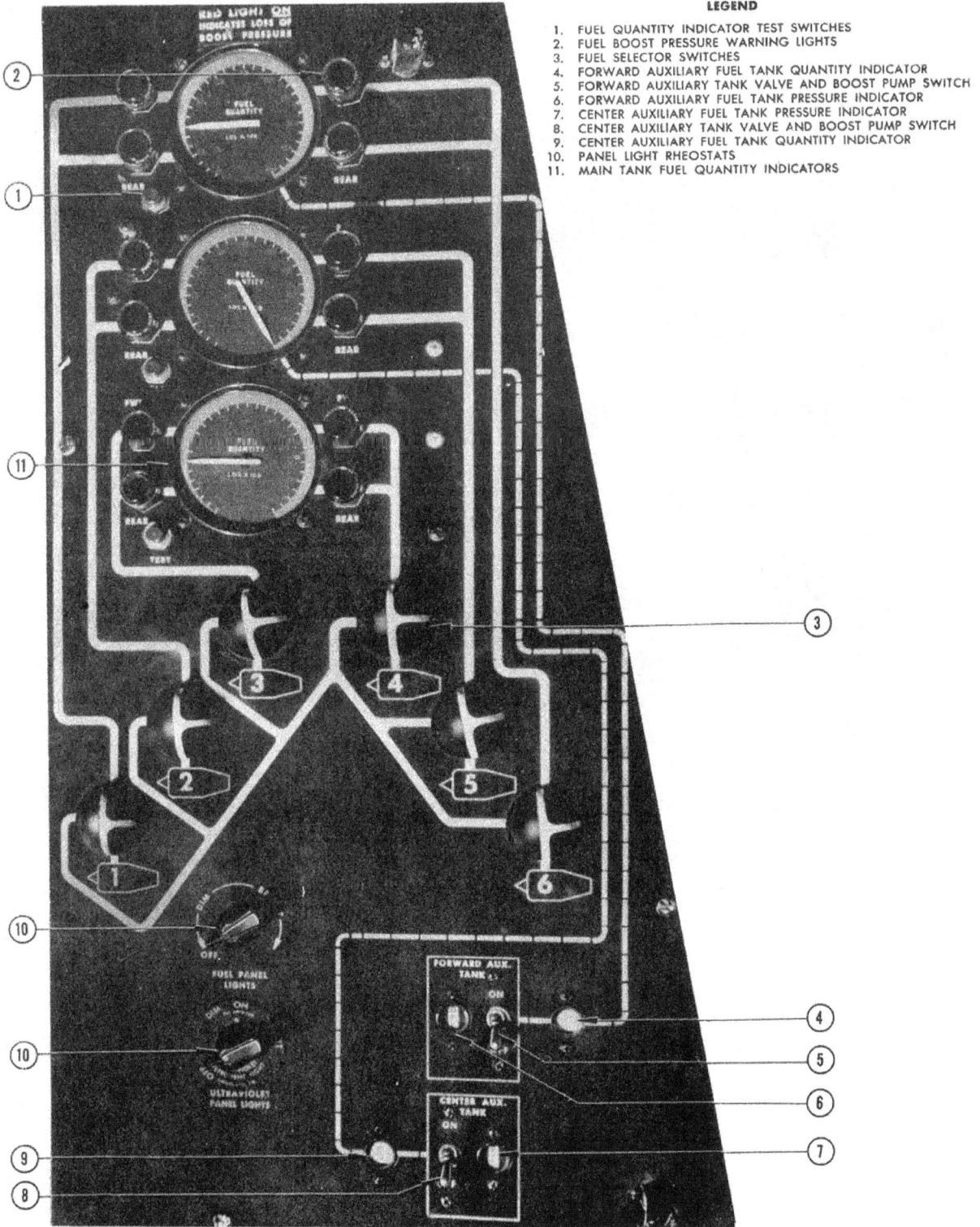

Figure 1-12. Fuel Control Panel

048038

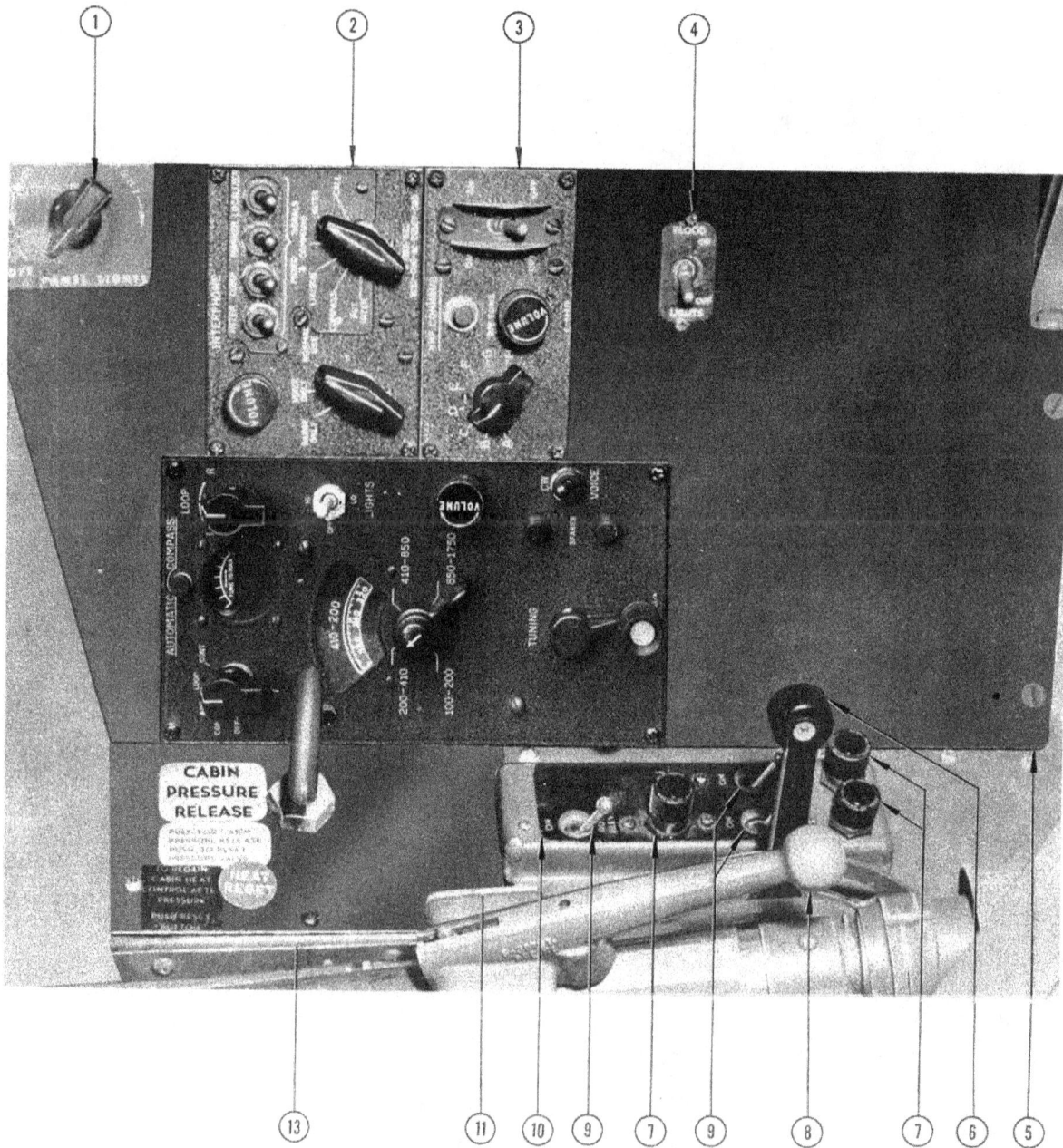

LEGEND

1. PANEL LIGHT RHEOSTAT
2. VHF COMMAND RADIO
3. INTERPHONE
4. COCKPIT LIGHT SWITCH
5. PILOT'S RADIO CONTROL PANEL
6. CANOPY CONTROL LEVER
7. SURFACE POWER CONTROL WARNING LIGHTS
8. CONTROL COLUMN LATCH LEVER
9. SURFACE POWER CONTROL SWITCHES
10. SURFACE POWER CONTROL PANEL
11. RADIO COMPASS
12. DELETED
13. EMERGENCY CABIN PRESSURE RELEASE HANDLE
14. HEAT RESET BUTTON

Figure 1-13. Pilot's Radio Control and Surface Power Control Panels

Revised 30 October 1950

① COPILOT'S INSTRUMENT PANEL ② MICROPHONE SWITCH ③ AUTOPILOT RELEASE SWITCH

Figure 1-14. Copilot's Station

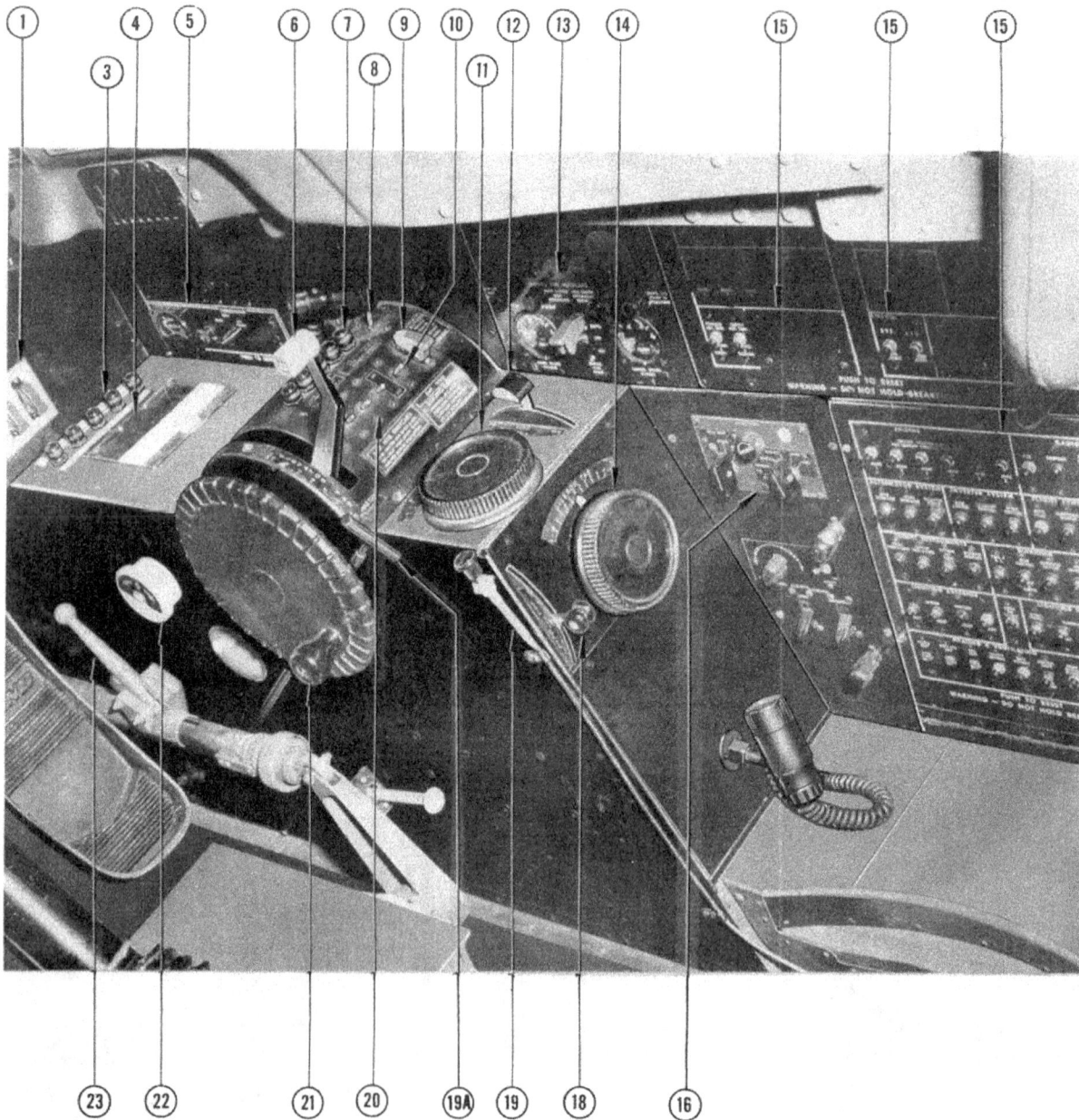

LEGEND

1. WING FLAP EMERGENCY SWITCHES
2. DELETED
3. LANDING GEAR WARNING LIGHTS
4. LANDING GEAR EMERGENCY RETRACTION SWITCHES
5. AC CIRCUIT BREAKER PANEL
6. MASTER THROTTLE
7. ANTI-ICING WARNING LIGHTS
8. WING OVERHEAT WARNING TEST SWITCH
9. WING ANTI-ICING CONTROL SWITCH
10. EMPENNAGE ANTI-ICING CONTROL SWITCH
11. RUDDER TRIM CONTROL KNOB AND INDICATOR
12. WING FLAP LEVER

13. HYDRAULIC CONTROL PANEL
14. AILERON TRIM CONTROL KNOB AND INDICATOR
15. COPILOT'S CIRCUIT BREAKER PANEL
16. COPILOT'S INTERPHONE CONTROL PANEL
17. DELETED
18. LANDING GEAR CONTROL LEVER
19. RUDDER PEDAL ADJUSTMENT KNOB
19A. DRAG CHUTE JETTISON HANDLE
20. EMPENNAGE HEATER SWITCHES
21. ELEVATOR TRIM CONTROL KNOB AND INDICATOR
22. HEAT SELECTOR KNOB
23. CONTROL COLUMN LATCH LEVER
24. DRAG CHUTE DEPLOYMENT HANDLE

Figure 1-15. Copilot's Station — Right Side

048041A

① PANEL LIGHT RHEOSTAT
② OXYGEN PRESSURE GAGE
③ OXYGEN FLOW INDICATOP
④ LANDING GEAR WARNING LIGHTS

⑤ LANDING GEAR EMERGENCY EXTENSION LEVER
⑥ LANDING GEAR EMERGENCY EXTENSION SELECTOR LEVERS

Figure 1-16. Copilot's Gunnery Station

048042A

① SUIT HEATER RECEPTACLES
② SUIT HEATER RHEOSTAT
③ WALKWAY DOME AND ENTRANCE LIGHTS SWITCH

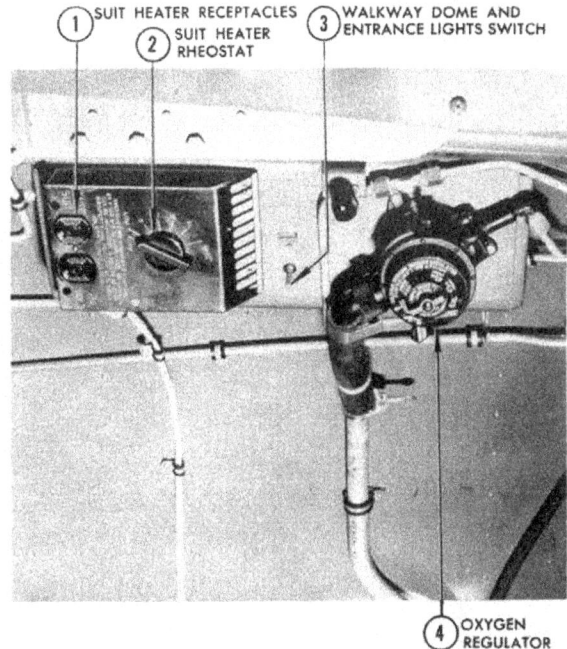

④ OXYGEN REGULATOR

Figure 1-17. Copilot's Station — Left Side

048043A

1-31. FUEL SPECIFICATION AND GRADE. The fuel used in this airplane shall conform to Specification MIL-F-5624, Grade JP-3 (recommended); Specification MIL-F-5616, Grade JP-1 (alternate); or Specification MIL-F-5572 (alternate). For ground ambient temperatures below -35° C (-30° F), only Specification MIL-F-5624 and Specification MIL-F-5572 fuel should be used.

NOTE

Any grade of fuel, Specification MIL-F-5572, may be used; however, the lowest grade available is recommended for economy reasons.

1-32. CONTROLS.

1-33. FUEL SELECTOR SWITCHES. Six rotary-type fuel selector switches (3, figure 1-12) on the fuel control panel provide a means of selecting the supply of fuel from any tank and/or the manifold for any engine. Switch positions are indicated on the panel by a schematic diagram of the courses of fuel flow. These positions are "Tank-to-Engine," "Tank-to-Engine and Manifold," and "Manifold-to-Engine." When the switches are in the "Tank-to-Engine" position, the fuel tank valves will be opened and the boost pumps energized as soon as the throttles are advanced out of "CUTOFF." When the switches are in the "Tank-to-Engine and Manifold" position, the fuel tank valves are opened, the boost pumps energized, and the manifold valves opened regardless of throttle position. When the switches are in the "Manifold-to-Engine" position, the manifold valves are opened regardless of throttle position. The fuel boost warning lights are energized as soon as a tank is selected regardless of throttle position.

Figure 1-18. Copilot's Instrument Panel

LEGEND

1. EMERGENCY CANOPY RELEASE HANDLE
2. OXYGEN FLOW INDICATOR
3. OXYGEN PRESSURE GAGE
4. TACHOMETERS
5. GYROSYN COMPASS
6. CLOCK
7. ATTITUDE GYRO
8. TURN-AND-BANK
9. MAXIMUM ALLOWABLE AIRSPEED INDICATOR
10. ALTIMETER
11. RATE-OF-CLIMB

12. WING FLAP POSITION INDICATOR
13. DC VOLTMETER
14. DC VOLTMETER SELECTOR SWITCH
15. DC LOADMETERS
16. GENERATOR OVERVOLTAGE LIGHTS
17. GENERATOR SWITCHES
18. GENERATOR VOLTAGE RHEOSTAT GUARD
19. INVERTER INDICATOR LIGHTS
20. INVERTER SWITCHES
21. AC VOLTMETER SELECTOR SWITCH
22. AC VOLTMETER

1-34. AUXILIARY TANK VALVE AND BOOST PUMP SWITCHES. Two "ON--OFF" switches (5, 8, figure 1-12) on the fuel control panel are used to electrically open the auxiliary fuel tank valves and energize the auxiliary fuel tank boost pumps. Overfilling of the main tanks from the auxiliary tanks is prevented by float switches in the circuit. Protection is provided by circuit breakers on the copilot's circuit breaker panel (3, figure 1-24).

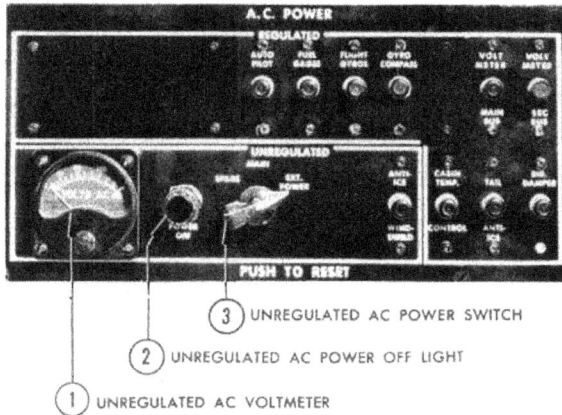

3 UNREGULATED AC POWER SWITCH

2 UNREGULATED AC POWER OFF LIGHT

1 UNREGULATED AC VOLTMETER

048045 A

Figure 1-19. AC Circuit Breaker Panel

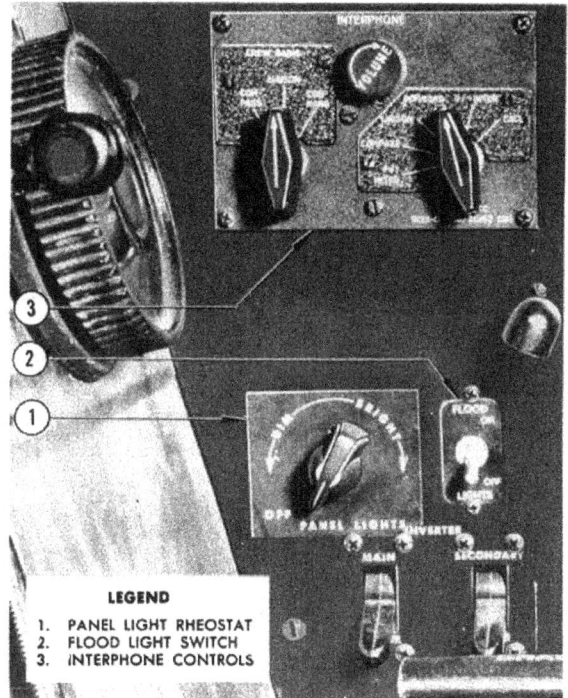

LEGEND
1. PANEL LIGHT RHEOSTAT
2. FLOOD LIGHT SWITCH
3. INTERPHONE CONTROLS

048047

Figure 1-21. Copilot's Interphone Control Panel

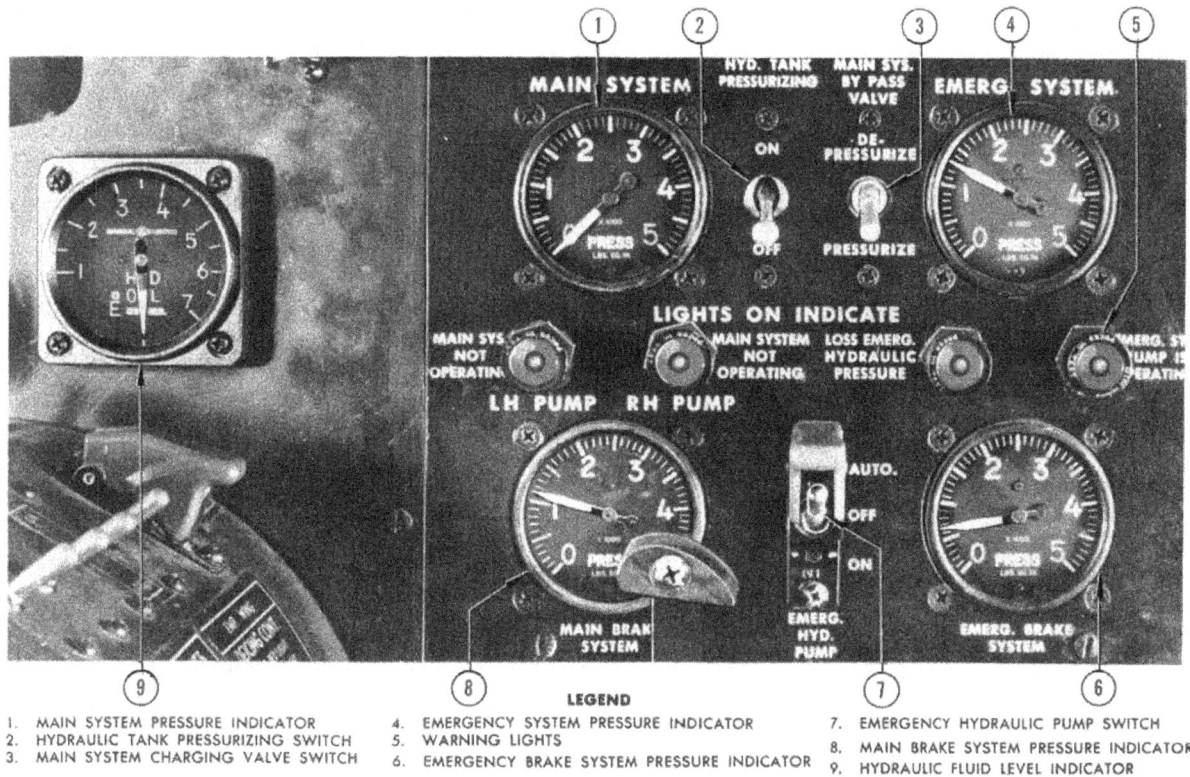

LEGEND

1. MAIN SYSTEM PRESSURE INDICATOR
2. HYDRAULIC TANK PRESSURIZING SWITCH
3. MAIN SYSTEM CHARGING VALVE SWITCH
4. EMERGENCY SYSTEM PRESSURE INDICATOR
5. WARNING LIGHTS
6. EMERGENCY BRAKE SYSTEM PRESSURE INDICATOR
7. EMERGENCY HYDRAULIC PUMP SWITCH
8. MAIN BRAKE SYSTEM PRESSURE INDICATOR
9. HYDRAULIC FLUID LEVEL INDICATOR

Figure 1-20. Hydraulic Control Panel

048046 A

TANKS	NO.	USABLE FUEL	UNUSABLE FUEL	EXPANSION SPACE	TOTAL VOLUME
FORWARD MAIN	1	16,159	174	440	16,660
FORWARD AUXILIARY	1	3,660	16	113	3,771
CENTER MAIN	1	18,434	391	830	19,010
CENTER AUXILIARY	1	3,081	8	93	3,179
REAR MAIN	1	22,282	168	950	22,970

USABLE FUEL TOTALS

MAIN TANKS   46,856
MAIN TANKS AND FORWARD AUXILIARY TANK   50,525
MAIN TANKS AND BOTH AUXILIARY TANKS   53,606

NOTE

Quantities are based on MIL-F-5624 fuel at 6.5 lbs. per gallon; unusable fuel includes the fuel in the lines.

Figure 1-22. Fuel Quantity Data (Lbs.)

048010A

1-35. INDICATORS.

1-36. FUEL QUANTITY INDICATORS. Three quantity indicators (11, figure 1-12) on the fuel control panel, show the fuel quantity in pounds for the main fuel tanks. Circuit breakers for the indicating circuits are on the AC circuit breaker panel (2, figure 1-24).

1-37. FUEL PRESSURE INDICATORS. Fuel pressure at each engine is indicated by six fuel pressure indicators (27, figure 1-8) on the pilot's instrument panel.

1-38. AUXILIARY FUEL TANK QUANTITY AND PRESSURE INDICATORS. Four tab-window type indicators (4, 6, 7, 9, figure 1-12) on the fuel control panel show, by interchangeable tabs, the condition of fuel quantity and pressure for the two auxiliary tanks. A full auxiliary tank is indicated by an "F" tab, an empty tank by an "E" tab, and all intermediate quantities by a divided black and white circle tab. No pressure from an auxiliary tank is indicated by an "OFF" tab, low pressure by a "LP" tab, and normal pressure by a "P" tab. The quantity indicating circuits are energized when power is on the airplane. The pressure indicating circuits are energized through the auxiliary tank valve and boost pump switches.

1-39. FUEL BOOST PRESSURE WARNING LIGHTS. Twelve fuel boost pressure warning lights (2, figure 1-12) for the main fuel tank pressure lines are provided on the fuel control panel. The lights will illuminate when the corresponding fuel selector switch is set to a tank and a low pressure exists in the line. The fuel boost pressure warning light circuits are protected by circuit breakers on the copilot's circuit breaker panel (3, figure 1-24).

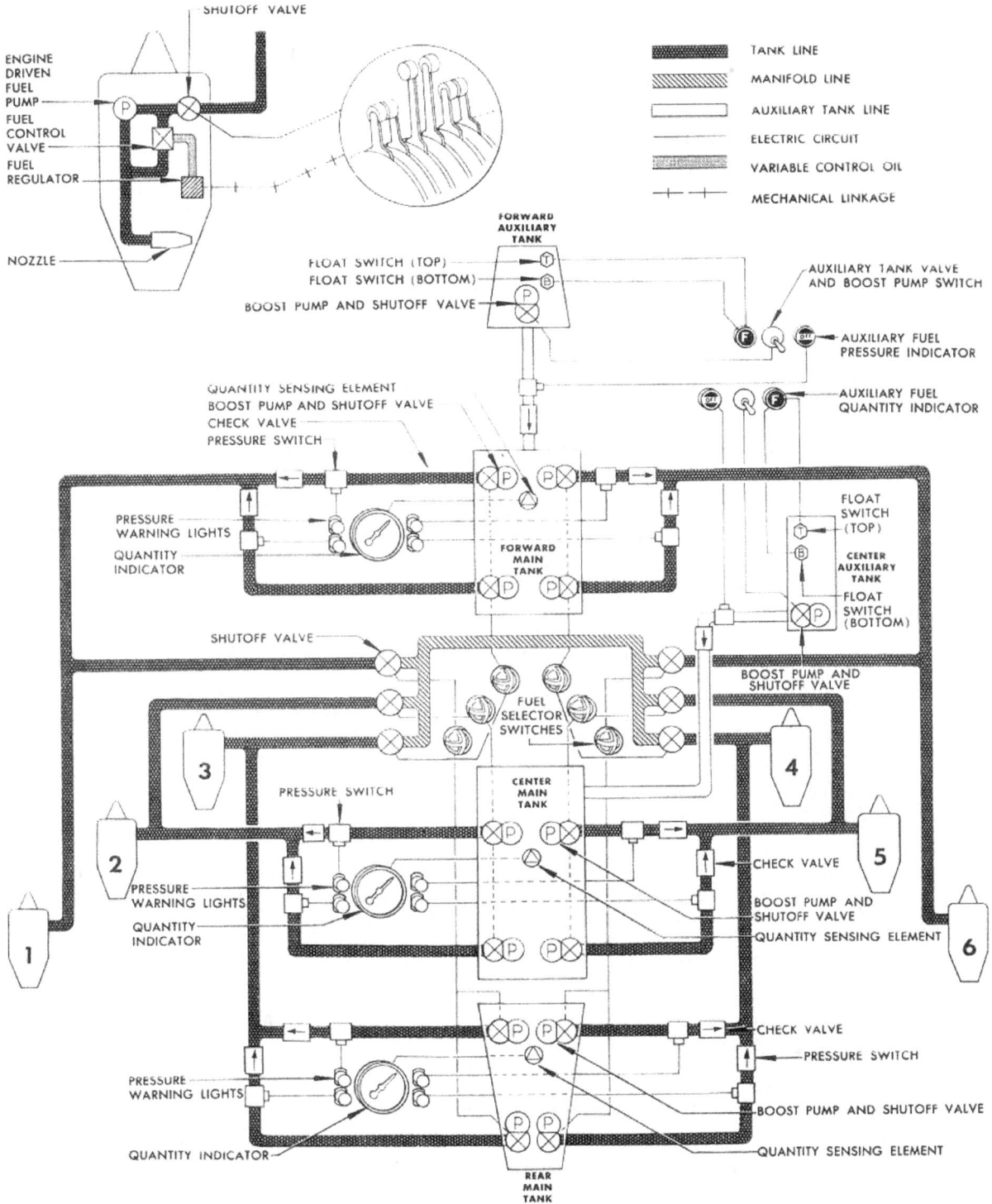

Figure 1-23. Fuel System

CIRCUIT	PANEL	CIRCUIT	PANEL	CIRCUIT	PANEL
Alternator Power Selector	3	Fuel and Oil Pressure Indicators (Engine No. 4)	1	Inverter, Secondary	5
Alternator Regulator, Main	3	Fuel and Oil Pressure		Landing Gear, Main	3
Alternator Regulator, Main	4	Indicators (Engine No. 5)	1	Landing Gear, Outrigger	3
Alternator Regulator, Spare	3	Fuel and Oil Pressure		Landing Gear Position	
Alternator Regulator, Spare	4	Indicators (Engine No. 6)	1	Warning	3
Anti-icing, Pitot and		Fuel Control, Main (Engine		Landing Gear Retraction,	
Windshield	3	No. 1)	3	Emergency	3
Anti-icing, Tail	2	Fuel Control, Main (Engine		Lights, Cabin Dome	3
Anti-icing, Tail	3	No. 2)	3	Lights, Copilot's and	
Anti-icing, Windshield	2	Fuel Control, Main (Engine		Navigator's Fluorescent	3
Anti-icing, Windshield	4	No. 3)	3	Lights, Flashing Position	3
Anti-icing, Wing	3	Fuel Control, Main (Engine		Lights, Flood	3
Anti-skid	3	No. 4)	3	Light, Left Landing	3
ATO Power Control	3	Fuel Control, Main (Engine		Lights, Panel	3
Autopilot	2	No. 5)	3	Lights, Pilot's Fluorescent	3
Autopilot	3	Fuel Control, Main (Engine		Light, Right Landing	3
Cabin Air Temperature		No. 6)	3	Lights, Spot	3
Control	3	Fuel Gages	2	Lights, Steady Position	3
Cabin Air Valves	3	Fuel Tank, Forward Auxil-		Lights, Tunnel Dome	3
Cabin Temperature Control	2	iary, Control and Warning	3	Nacelle Air Shutoff Door	
Defrosting, Canopy	3	Fuel Tank, Center Auxiliary,		(No. 1)	1
Defrosting, Nose	3	Control and Warning	3	Nacelle Air Shutoff Door	
Directional Damper	2	Fuel Warning, Main		(No. 2)	1
Directional Damper	3	(Engine No. 1)	3	Nacelle Air Shutoff Door	
Engine Control (No. 1)	3	Fuel Warning, Main		(No. 3)	1
Engine Control (No. 2)	3	(Engine No. 2)	3	Nacelle Air Shutoff Door	
Engine Control (No. 3)	3	Fuel Warning, Main		(No. 4)	1
Engine Control (No. 4)	3	(Engine No. 3)	3	Nacelle Air Shutoff Door	
Engine Control (No. 5)	3	Fuel Warning, Main		(No. 5)	1
Engine Control (No. 6)	3	(Engine No. 4)	3	Nacelle Air Shutoff Door	
Fire Detection Warning	3	Fuel Warning, Main		(No. 6)	1
Flap Control, Emergency		(Engine No. 5)	3	Radar Bombing, Navigation-	
(Primary Motor)	3	Fuel Warning, Main		al, and Computing Systems	6
Flap Control, Emergency		(Engine No. 6)	3	Radio Compass	3
Alternate (Secondary		Ground Blower, Cabin	3	Suit Heater, Copilot's	3
Motor)	3	Gyrosyn Compass	2	Suit Heat, Navigator's	3
Flap Control, Normal	3	Gyrosyn Compass	3	Suit Heater, Pilot's	3
Flap Position Indicator	3	Hydraulic Standby Control	3	Surface Boost	3
Flight Gyros	2	Hydraulic Oil Quantity	3	Temperature, Outside Air	3
Fuel and AC Warning	3	Hydraulic Warning	3	Turn-and-Bank, Copilot's	3
Fuel and Oil Pressure		Interphone	3	Turn-and-Bank, Pilot's	3
Indicators (Engine No. 1)	1	Inverter Control, Main	3	Vibrators, Instrument Panel	3
Fuel and Oil Pressure		Inverter Control, Secondary	3	Voltmeter, Main Bus	2
Indicators (Engine No. 2)	1	Inverter Control, Spare	3	Voltmeter, Secondary Bus	2
Fuel and Oil Pressure		Inverter, Main	5	Voltmeter, Unregulated AC	4
Indicators (Engine No. 3)	1				

LEGEND

1. MAIN AC POWER SHIELD
2. AC CIRCUIT BREAKER PANEL
3. COPILOT'S CIRCUIT BREAKER PANEL
4. UNREGULATED AC POWER SHIELD
5. COPILOT'S INTERPHONE CONTROL PANEL
6. RADAR POWER PANEL

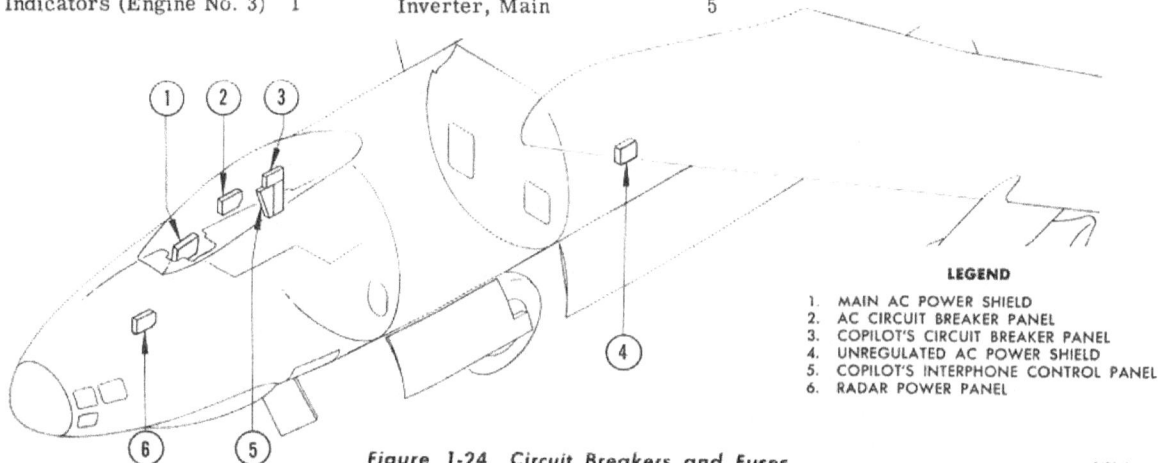

Figure 1-24. Circuit Breakers and Fuses

048011 A

1-40. ELECTRICAL SYSTEM.

1-41. GENERAL.

1-42. DIRECT CURRENT SYSTEM. Direct current power is provided by six 28-volt engine-driven generators. The system is primarily a ground return, single conductor type, except where it is necessary to use two conductors to avoid magnetic deviation. The generators are combination starter-generator units, acting as starters for cranking the engines up to approximately 25% RPM, and thereafter operating as generators. Two 12-volt storage batteries connected in series provide a stand-by power source and may be used for emergency starting of engines only when external power is not available. All electrical equipment and systems, except fuel quantity, fuel and oil pressure, and flight gyro indicating systems, require direct current power for their control or operation. Suit heater receptacles and rheostats are on the oxygen panels at each crew station. Suit heater circuit breakers are on the copilot's circuit breaker panel (3, figure 1-24).

1-43. REGULATED ALTERNATING CURRENT SYSTEM. Regulated 115-volt 400-cycle alternating current is supplied to a main and secondary bus system by three single-phase inverters. One inverter is a spare which will automatically operate, or can be manually selected, to supply power to either bus in the event of failure of the main or secondary inverter. However, if the spare inverter is being used for the main bus load, it cannot be used automatically or manually for the secondary load. Phase adapters provide 115-volt, three-phase power, while 26-volt single-phase power is supplied through a transformer. The following equipment requires regulated alternating current for its control or operation: autopilot; directional damper; nacelle air close-off doors (engines, 2, 3, 4, and 5 only); cabin heating and pressurizing control; empennage anti-icing; gyrosyn compass; flight gyros; fuel quantity, fuel and oil pressure indicating systems; and radar equipment. Some airplanes also have an additional 115-volt three-phase inverter to supply 400-cycle regulated alternating current for some radar equipment.

1-44. UNREGULATED ALTERNATING CURRENT SYSTEM. Unregulated 115-volt alternating current is supplied by one of two engine-driven alternators. The main alternator is driven by the No. 1 engine and the spare alternator is driven by the No. 6 engine. Unregulated alternating current is used for windshield deicing and some radar equipment.

1-45. CONTROLS.

1-46. BATTERY SWITCH. The "ON--OFF" battery switch (12, figure 1-11) is located on the pilot's switch panel. The "ON" position of the switch energizes a battery-disconnect relay which connects the batteries to the DC power bus. The "OFF" position causes the relay to be de-energized thus disconnecting the batteries from the power bus.

1-47. GENERATOR SWITCHES. Six individual generator switches (17, figure 1-18) are on the copilot's instrument panel. The switches are marked "ON--OFF--RESET" and are guarded to the "ON" position. When a switch is in the "ON" position, the generator is delivering power to the direct current bus, provided that the generator voltage is sufficiently high. In the "OFF" position, the switch prevents the reverse current relay from connecting the generator to the bus as a generator. The "RESET" position of the switch is used to reset the field relay to restore generator operation after the field relay has been tripped by generator overvoltage or fire button actuation. When in the "RESET" position, the switch is spring-loaded to "OFF."

1-48. GENERATOR VOLTAGE RHEOSTATS. Six generator voltage rheostats are behind a hinged cover guard (18, figure 1-18), below the generator switches, on the copilot's instrument panel. The rheostats are to be used only for adjusting generator voltages to equalize generator load distribution.

1-49. INVERTER SWITCHES. Two switches (20, figure 1-18) on the copilot's instrument panel control the main, secondary, and spare inverters. The switch for the main regulated AC bus is marked "MAIN INVERTER--OFF--SPARE INVERTER." With the switch in the "MAIN INVERTER" position, the main inverter is energized through an automatic change-over relay to supply alternating current to the main AC bus. If the main inverter should fail to supply power to the main AC bus when the switch is in this position, the automatic change-over relay will start the spare inverter and connect it to the main bus. Also, the spare inverter output will be transferred to the main bus if the spare inverter is being used to supply power to the secondary bus. When the switch is in the "OFF" position, the main inverter, or the spare inverter if operating for the main bus, will be de-energized and disconnected from the main bus. The "SPARE INVERTER" position provides a manual control of the spare inverter for main bus operation in the event that the automatic change-over relay fails to operate. The switch for the secondary bus is marked "SECONDARY INVERTER--OFF--SPARE INVERTER." With the switch in the "SECONDARY INVERTER" position, the secondary inverter is energized through another automatic change-over relay to supply alternating current to the secondary AC bus. If the secondary inverter should fail to supply power to the secondary bus when the switch is in this position, and the spare inverter is not being used to supply power to the main AC bus, the automatic change-over relay will start the spare inverter and connect it to the secondary bus. When the switch is in the "OFF" position, the secondary inverter, or the spare inverter, if operating for the secondary bus, will be de-energized and disconnected from the secondary bus. The "SPARE INVERTER" position provides a manual control of the spare inverter for secondary bus operation, in the event that the automatic change-over relay fails to operate and the spare inverter is not being used for main bus operation.

1-50. On airplanes using an additional 115-volt 400-cycle three-phase inverter, the "ON--OFF" control

048077

switch for the K-2 radar power system is located on the bomb primary control assembly support panel at the navigator's station. When the switch is in the "ON" position, an inverter control relay is energized to supply DC power to operate the inverter to supply regulated AC power. When the switch is in the "OFF" position, the control relay is de-energized causing the inverter to be off.

1-51. Control circuit breakers for the single-phase inverter system are on the copilot's circuit breaker panel (3, figure 1-24) and switch-type circuit breakers for the main and secondary inverters are on the copilot's interphone control panel (5, figure 1-24). The control circuit breaker for the three-phase inverter is on the radar power panel (6, figure 1-24).

1-52. UNREGULATED AC POWER SWITCH. A single rotary type switch (3, figure 1-19) on the AC circuit breaker panel is used to select the 115-volt unregulated alternating current power source. The switch positions are marked "SPARE--MAIN--EXT POWER." When the switch is in the "SPARE" position, the output of the No. 6 engine-driven alternator is connected to the unregulated AC power bus. In the "MAIN" position, the output of the No. 1 engine-driven alternator is connected to the unregulated AC power bus. When the switch is in the "EXT POWER" position, the AC external power receptacle is connected to the unregulated AC power bus if an external source of AC power is plugged into the receptacle. Unregulated power system circuit breakers are on the copilot's circuit breaker panel (3, figure 1-24).

1-53. DC VOLTMETER SELECTOR SWITCH. A rotary type switch (14, figure 1-18) on the copilot's instrument panel provides a means of obtaining individual generator and direct current bus voltage readings on a single voltmeter. The switch is marked "OFF--1--2--3--4--5--6--BUS." In the "OFF" position the switch disconnects the voltmeter from any power source. In the "1" through "6" positions, the switch connects the voltmeter to the corresponding generator to indicate individual generator voltage. When the selector switch is in the "BUS" position, the voltmeter is connected to the DC power bus system.

1-54. AC VOLTMETER SELECTOR SWITCH. A toggle switch (21, figure 1-18) on the copilot's instrument panel, with positions marked "MAIN BUS--SECONDARY BUS," connects the regulated AC voltmeter to the bus corresponding to the toggle position. The regulated AC voltmeter circuit breakers are on the AC circuit breaker panel (2, figure 1-24).

1-55. EXTERNAL POWER RECEPTACLES. Two direct current and one unregulated alternating current external receptacles (9, figure 1-4) are located in the lower left side of the fuselage just aft of the forward main wheel well. A hinged access door is provided to cover the receptacles.

1-56. CIRCUIT BREAKERS AND FUSES. Push-pull, push-to-reset, and switch-type circuit breakers, as well as fuses protect the individual circuits from overload. These circuit breakers and fuses are located on the main AC power shield, AC circuit breaker panel, copilot's circuit breaker panel, unregulated AC power shield, copilot's interphone control panel, and the radar power panel (1, 2, 3, 4, 5, 6, figure 1-24).

1-57. INDICATORS.

1-58. GENERATOR OVERVOLTAGE LIGHTS. Six generator overvoltage lights (16, figure 1-18) on the copilot's instrument panel indicate, when on, that a generator field relay has been tripped because of high generator voltage or the fire button has been actuated with the corresponding throttle lever at cutoff. To reset the field relay, the individual generator switch must be momentarily actuated to the "RESET" position.

1-59. DC VOLTMETER. A single direct current voltmeter is used to indicate individual generator or bus voltage. The voltmeter (13, figure 1-18) is located on the copilot's instrument panel and is connected to the individual generator or the bus through a rotary type selector switch.

1-60. DC LOADMETERS. Six direct current loadmeters (15, figure 1-18) are on the copilot's instrument panel and are used to indicate individual generator load. The loadmeters are calibrated in per cent of rated generator load.

1-61. INVERTER INDICATOR LIGHTS. Two lights are used to indicate regulated AC power main bus conditions. An amber light will be on when the spare inverter is ready to supply power to the main bus. A red light will be on when the main and spare inverters fail to supply power to the main bus or when the inverter switch for the main bus is in the "OFF" position. An additional amber light is used for the regulated AC power secondary bus to indicate, when on, that the spare inverter is on to supply power to the secondary bus. The inverter indicator lights (19, figure 1-18) are on the copilot's instrument panel.

1-62. REGULATED AC VOLTMETER. A single alternating current voltmeter (22, figure 1-18) on the copilot's instrument panel indicates main or secondary regulated AC bus voltage. The voltmeter is connected to the main or secondary bus by means of a toggle-type selector switch. Regulated AC voltmeter circuit breakers are located on the AC circuit breaker panel (2, figure 1-25).

1-63. UNREGULATED AC POWER OFF LIGHT. A red light (2, figure 1-19), on the AC circuit breaker panel will be on whenever there is no unregulated AC power being supplied to the unregulated AC power bus by either the engine-driven alternators or an external power source. The unregulated AC power warning light circuit breaker is located on the copilot's circuit breaker panel (3, figure 1-24).

1-64. UNREGULATED AC VOLTMETER. One AC voltmeter (1, figure 1-19) on the AC circuit breaker panel indicates unregulated AC power bus voltage. The voltmeter circuit breaker is on the unregulated AC power shield (4, figure 1-24).

1-65. HYDRAULIC SYSTEM.

1-66. GENERAL.

1-66A. There are two major hydraulic systems and three minor hydraulic systems. The two major systems, main and emergency, supply pressure to operate the front gear steering, brakes, canopy, and bomb doors (figure 1-25). Shuttle valves interconnect the two major systems and allow the system with the highest pressure to supply the actuating units. The minor systems operate the surface power controls.

1-67. MAIN SYSTEM. The main system incorporates a 4 1/2 U.S. gallon reservoir in a 9 U.S. gallon system. The reservoir supplies engine-driven pumps on engines No. 3 and No. 4. A fire shutoff valve in each pump supply line is closed when the throttle for the corresponding engine is placed in "CUTOFF" and a fire button (11, figure 1-8) on the pilot's instrument panel is pushed. Moving the throttle out of "CUTOFF" opens the shutoff valve. The two engine-driven pumps are set to maintain 3000 PSI, and a check valve in each pump pressure line prevents loss of pressure in the event one pump becomes inoperative. When the main landing gear retracts, it actuates an automatic by-pass valve which depressurizes the front gear steering system, and makes possible the depressurization of the entire main system. The system is depressurized by operating the main system charging valve. Extension of the landing gear closes the automatic by-pass valve and pressurizes the main system.

1-68. EMERGENCY SYSTEM. The emergency system provides pressure to operate the front gear steering, brakes, canopy, and bomb doors independent of the main system pumps and lines. A 1 3/4 U.S. gallon reservoir supplies an electrically driven pump which provides 3000 PSI to operate the emergency system. During emergency operation, return flow is automatically directed to the emergency reservoir. Shuttle valves automatically direct emergency system pressure to the actuating units whenever emergency system pressure is greater than main system pressure. Depressurizing the main system does not affect pressures in the emergency system.

1-69. CONTROLS.

1-70. HYD. TANK PRESSURIZING SWITCH. A circuit-breaker type "ON--OFF" switch (2, figure 1-20) is on the copilot's hydraulic control panel. When the switch is "ON," an electrically driven air pump is energized to pressurize the main and emergency system reservoirs. Pressurizing the reservoirs prevents foaming of the hydraulic fluid. When the switch is "OFF," the reservoirs are not pressurized.

1-71. MAIN SYSTEM CHARGING VALVE SWITCH. This switch (3, figure 1-20) is on the copilot's hydraulic control panel. When the landing gear is retracted, an automatic by-pass valve (figure 1-25) is opened, permitting the main system to be depressurized by placing the charging valve switch in the "DEPRESSURIZE" position. Main system pressure is built up by placing the switch in the "PRESSURIZE" position. The switch controls a system charging valve (figure 1-25) in the main system pressure lines. Extension of the landing gear closes the automatic by-pass valve and builds up system pressure automatically, even though the charging valve switch may be in the "DEPRESSURIZE" position. A circuit breaker for this switch is on the copilot's circuit breaker panel (3, figure 1-24). A similar switch (13, figure 4-8) is on the bombardier's panel.

1-72. EMERGENCY HYDRAULIC PUMP SWITCH. The emergency system pump is controlled by a guarded "AUTO--OFF--ON" switch (7, figure 1-20) on the copilot's hydraulic control panel. When the switch is in the "AUTO" position, the electrically operated pump (figure 1-25) maintains emergency system pressure between 2700 and 3000 PSI. When the switch is held in the spring-loaded "ON" position, a pressure switch is by-passed and pressures up to the maximum are built up. When the switch is in the "OFF" position, no emergency system pressure will be built up. A circuit breaker for the switch, marked standby control, is on the copilot's circuit breaker panel (3, figure 1-24).

1-73. INDICATORS.

1-74. MAIN SYSTEM PRESSURE INDICATOR. The main system pressure indicator (1, figure 1-20), on the copilot's hydraulic control panel, is connected directly to the main system lines (figure 1-25), and indicates pressure available to the actuating units.

1-75. EMERGENCY SYSTEM PRESSURE INDICATOR. A pressure indicator (4, figure 1-20) on the copilot's hydraulic control panel is connected directly to the air side of the emergency system accumulator (figure 1-25). Emergency system pressure is not available to the shuttle valves until the indication is greater than the minimum value.

1-76. HYDRAULIC FLUID LEVEL INDICATOR. Fluid level in the main system hydraulic reservoir is indicated on an instrument on the copilot's side wall panel (9, figure 1-20). A circuit breaker for the hydraulic fluid level indicator is on the copilot's circuit breaker panel (3, figure 1-24). A sight gage is provided on the hydraulic tank in the forward wheel well.

1-77. WARNING LIGHTS. Four warning lights are on the copilot's hydraulic control panel (5, figure 1-20). Three of the lights are connected to pressure switches (figure 1-25) in the outlet lines from the main system pumps and the emergency system pump. When pressure from a main pump falls below 2200 PSI, a light is illuminated. The fourth light is illuminated when the emergency pump is operating. 048079A

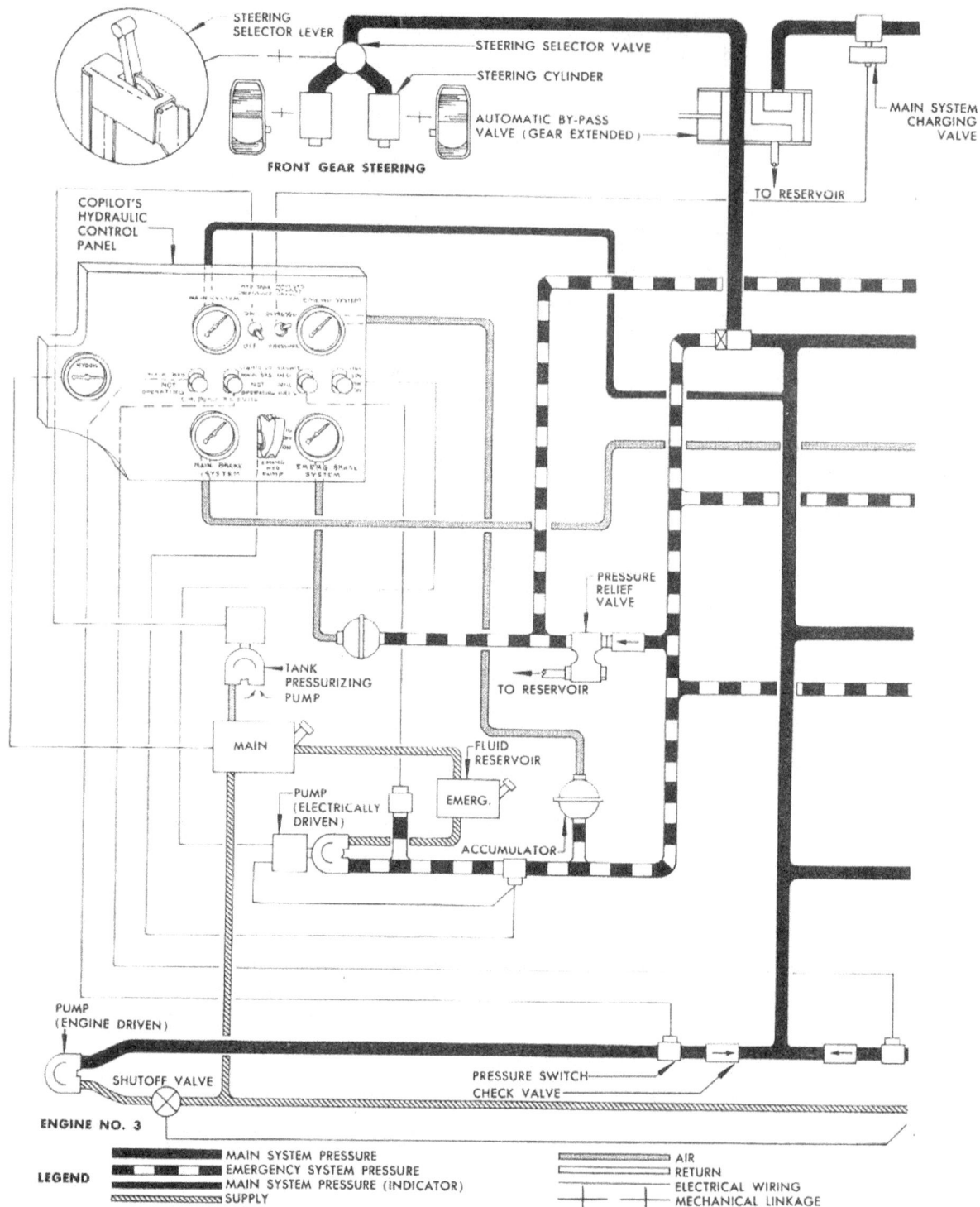

STEERING
SELECTOR LEVER

STEERING SELECTOR VALVE

STEERING CYLINDER

AUTOMATIC BY-PASS
VALVE (GEAR EXTENDED)

MAIN SYSTEM
CHARGING
VALVE

FRONT GEAR STEERING

TO RESERVOIR

COPILOT'S
HYDRAULIC
CONTROL
PANEL

PRESSURE
RELIEF
VALVE

TANK
PRESSURIZING
PUMP

TO RESERVOIR

MAIN

FLUID
RESERVOIR

PUMP
(ELECTRICALLY
DRIVEN)

EMERG.

ACCUMULATOR

PUMP
(ENGINE DRIVEN)

SHUTOFF VALVE

PRESSURE SWITCH
CHECK VALVE

ENGINE NO. 3

LEGEND

MAIN SYSTEM PRESSURE	AIR
EMERGENCY SYSTEM PRESSURE	RETURN
MAIN SYSTEM PRESSURE (INDICATOR)	ELECTRICAL WIRING
SUPPLY	MECHANICAL LINKAGE

Figure 1-25. (Sheet 1 of 2 Sheets). Hydraulic System

048012 a A

1-78. FLIGHT CONTROL SYSTEM.

1-79. GENERAL.

1-79A. In this airplane hydraulic pressure is employed as the primary means of actuating the control surfaces, and since hydraulic actuation of the control surfaces relieves the pilot of all control pressures, artificial control pressure, or feel, is induced in the power control system to simulate normal control feel. A conventional cable system operates the power control system and also provides a means of manually operating the control surfaces if the power control system becomes inoperative. Sealed balances at the rudder, elevator, and aileron surfaces reduce the control forces required of the pilot when the surface power control system is not operating. Conventionally operated trim control is coordinated with surface power control in such a manner as to reduce adjustments when changing from surface power control on or off. Two trim tabs are provided for elevator trim. The left tab is actuated by the wing flaps to give automatic trimming to compensate for flap pitching moments. The right tab is operated by the pilot or copilot. An electrically operated directional damper has been incorporated in the rudder surface power control system to prevent directional oscillation during air speeds of less than approximately 347 knots IAS.

1-80. SURFACE POWER CONTROL SYSTEMS. Three surface power control systems supply hydraulic pressure to operate the rudder, elevators, and each aileron. The aileron power control systems also operate the flaperon. The power control systems are entirely independent of the main and emergency hydraulic systems; each power control system has separate fluid reservoirs, electrically driven pumps, surface actuators, and controls. A single system for rudder and elevator power control is in the empennage; each aileron and flaperon power control system is in its respective wing. The surface power control systems are operated by the pilot's and copilot's flight controls, and switches at the pilot's station. When the control surfaces are locked, the power control systems are automatically de-energized.

1-80A. DIRECTIONAL DAMPER. A directional damper system is provided which is essentially an autopilot acting on the rudder to counteract any yawing or rolling tendencies that might be encountered at high altitudes or low air speeds. When the system is turned on in level flight, no rudder actuation will occur. In a turn, the damper system is cut out to allow coordinated turns to be made.

1-81. WING FLAPS. The wing flaps are designed to provide high lift and low drag, and to operate with a minimum of pilot attention. The flaps are actuated in such a way as to give a fast extension, approximately 20 seconds, and a slow retraction, approximately 40 seconds (figure 1-25A). The slow retraction allows the airplane time to accelerate before the flaps reach the up position. If the flaps retract to the 20% down position before 175 knots IAS is reached, a ram-air pressure switch will prevent further retraction until

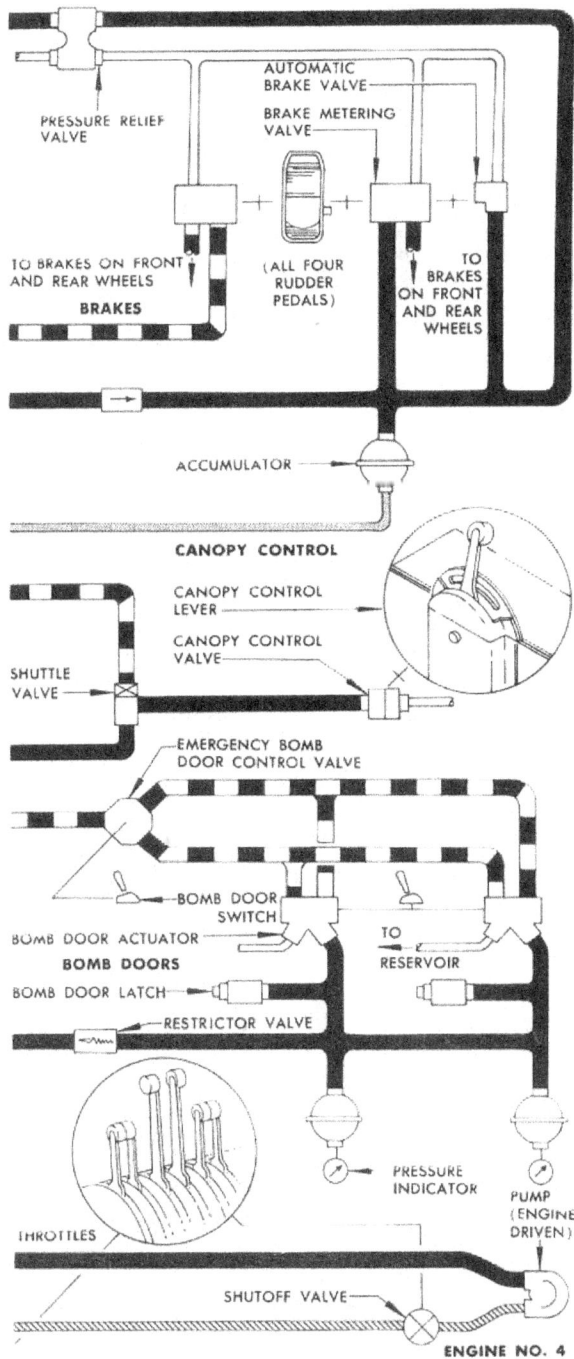

Figure 1-25 (Sheet 2 of 2 Sheets). Hydraulic System

048012b A

the required air speed is obtained; this prevents the airplane from sinking due to insufficient lift. The wing flaps also operate the left elevator trim tab.

1-82. SLATS. The slats, along the outer leading edge of the wing, provide a smooth air flow over the wing at low air speeds to give good stalling characteristics. The wing slats are operated automatically by the first 25% of wing flap movement. They extend and retract with the flaps. A warning horn will sound if the flaps and slats are retracted during low air speeds.

1-83. FLAPERONS. The outboard flap on each wing operates as a conventional flap with the additional feature of rotating upwards to supplement aileron action. The flaps must be fully extended to obtain flaperon action. Rotating an aileron upward from 6° up to maximum up will result in the corresponding flaperon moving upward from 35° down to 10° down. The left flaperon is hydraulically actuated by the surface power control system that operates the left aileron; the same is true of the right flaperon and aileron. Failure of an aileron power control system results in the corresponding flaperon fully extending to operate only as a conventional flap.

1-84. CONTROLS.

1-85. SURFACE POWER CONTROL SWITCHES. Hydraulic pressure to operate the flight control surfaces is selected for the left aileron (and flaperon), right aileron (and flaperon), rudder, and elevator by three "ON--off" switches (9, figure 1-13) on the surface power control panel at the pilot's station. A circuit breaker, marked surface boost, is on the copilot's circuit breaker panel (3, figure 1-24). Placing a surface power control switch to "ON" energizes the selected power control system, when placed in off, the power control system is de-energized and the surfaces are actuated manually.

1-86. DIRECTIONAL DAMPER SWITCH. A directional damper "ON--OFF" switch (5, figure 1-8) is on the pilot's instrument panel. A directional damper circuit breaker is on the copilot's circuit breaker panel (3, figure 1-24). Placing the switch in the "ON" position energizes the damper mechanism without any noticeable effect other than the more desirable flying characteristics. When the switch is in the "OFF" position, the directional damper is inoperative.

1-87. RUDDER PEDALS. The rudder pedals can be adjusted by pull knobs on the pilot's and copilot's control stands (16, figure 1-6 and 19, figure 1-15). When the knob is pulled up, the pedals spring to the aft position. When the pedals are moved to the desired position, and the knob is released, the pedals are latched in position. Movement of the pedals operates the front gear steering, and toe pressure on any one of the four pedals will actuate the brakes.

1-88. CONTROL COLUMN AND WHEEL. Pilot and copilot control columns can be disconnected and stowed in the forward position. Operation of a latch lever (8, figure 1-13 and 23, figure 1-15) on the control column push-rods disengages the control columns. Adjustment collars on the push-rods permits fore and aft adjustment of the control columns. Microphone and autopilot cutout switches are on the control wheels.

1-89. WING FLAP LEVERS. The wing flaps are normally controlled by levers (9, figure 1-6 and 12, figure 1-15) on the pilot's and copilot's control stands. The handle on each lever is in the shape of a miniature airfoil to facilitate easy recognition. The pilot's wing flap lever has notched "UP--OFF--DOWN" positions. The copilot's lever has similar positions but is not notched. Both wing flap levers are interconnected and controllable from either station. When the lever is in "UP," the flaps retract in approximately 40 seconds; when in "DOWN," the flaps extend in approximately 20 seconds. The flaps are held in any intermediate position by placing the lever in "OFF."

1-90. GROUND OPERATION FLAP SWITCH. Some airplanes have a ground operation flap switch on the copilot's circuit breaker panel (3, figure 1-24). The switch has "off--UP" positions and is guarded in off. Operation of the switch to "UP," retracts the flaps at twice the normal speed. This switch will operate the flaps regardless of normal wing flap lever position.

1-91. WING FLAP EMERGENCY SWITCHES. Two guarded "DOWN--OFF--UP" switches (1, figure 1-15) on the copilot's instrument panel, control the wing flap primary and secondary motors for emergency operation. These switches by-pass all limit, safety, ground operation, and control lever switches. When either switch is placed in "DOWN," both motors operate, and extend the flaps in approximately 20 seconds. When emergency retraction is desired, either the primary or secondary motor is selected by moving the corresponding switch to "UP." Placing one switch to "UP," retracts the flaps in approximately 40 seconds; placing both switches to "UP," retracts the flaps in approximately 20 seconds.

1-92. WING SLAT WARNING HORN SWITCH. A wing slat warning switch (10, figure 1-11) is on the pilot's switch panel. When the switch is in "NORMAL," a warning horn will sound if the flaps and slats are not extended below 175 knots IAS. The horn is prevented from sounding by placing the switch in "OFF."

1-93. TRIM CONTROL KNOBS AND INDICATORS. Conventional trim control knobs and indicators are on the pilot's and copilot's control stands (8, 11, 17, figure 1-6 and 11, 14, 21, figure 1-15).

1-94. SURFACE LOCK LEVER. A surface lock lever (6, figure 1-6) with "LOCK--UNLOCK" positions is on the pilot's control stand. The surfaces are locked by placing the lever in "LOCK" and operating the ailerons, elevators, and rudder until lock plungers seat and surface controls cannot be moved. Rudder and ailerons are locked in neutral, and elevators are locked in full down. The surface lock lever prevents throttles from being opened beyond 52% RPM when surfaces are locked. Surfaces cannot be locked if any throttle is open beyond 52% RPM. When the lock lever is in "LOCK," the surface power control

04B080A

WARNING

WITH EITHER MOTOR RUNNING, OUTPUT SHAFT RUNS AT HALF SPEED OF MOTOR; FLAPS RETRACT IN 40 SECONDS. WITH BOTH MOTORS RUNNING, OUTPUT SHAFT RUNS AT SAME SPEED AS MOTORS; FLAPS RETRACT IN 20 SECONDS. ONLY ONE MOTOR SHOULD BE USED FOR RETRACTION.

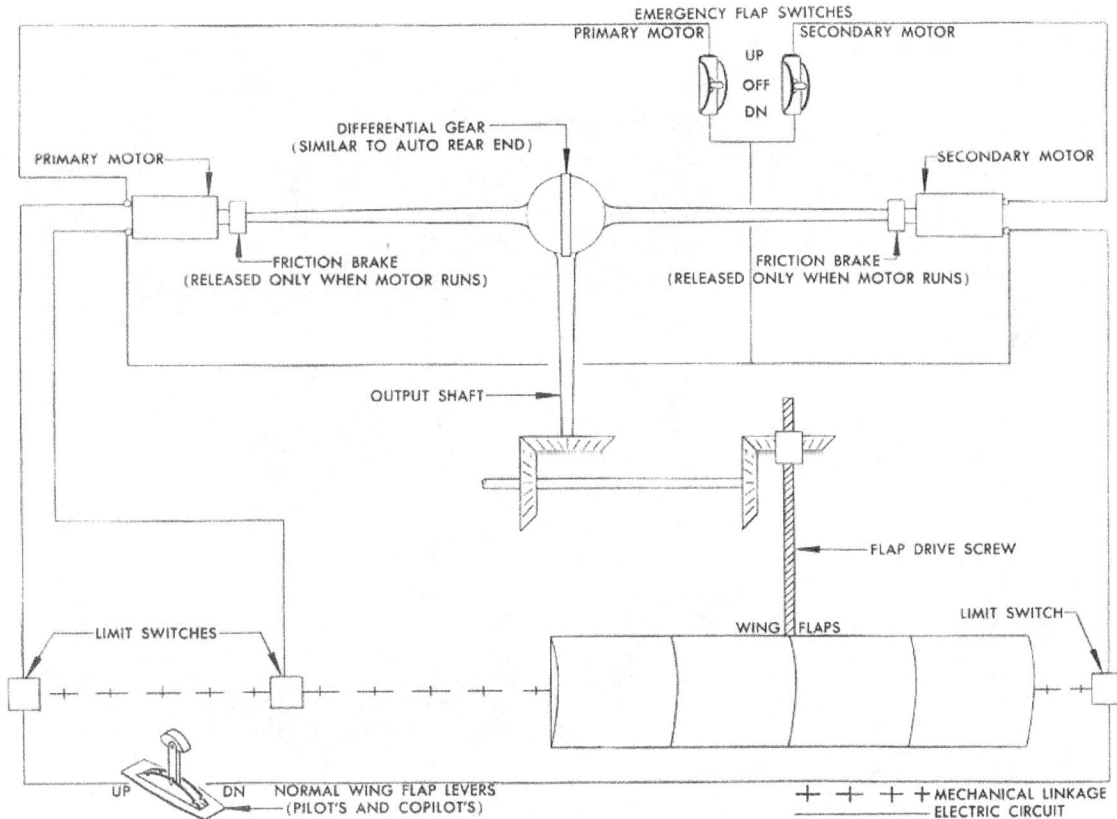

Figure 1-25A. Wing Flap Control System

systems are inoperative. When the lever is in "UNLOCK," all flight controls and throttles are unlocked, and the surface power control systems can be energized.

1-95. INDICATORS.

1-96. SURFACE POWER CONTROL WARNING LIGHTS. When hydraulic pressure in a surface power control system falls below 350 PSI, the system is automatically disconnected from the control surface, a low pressure warning light (7, figure 1-13) on the surface power control panel is lighted, and the control surface affected is then manually operated by the conventional cable system. Warning lights are provided for each of the three surface power control systems.

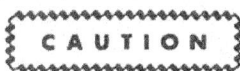

CAUTION

Considerable out of trim forces can occur when surface power control goes off.

1-97. WING FLAP POSITION INDICATOR. A wing flap position indicator (19, figure 1-8), on the pilot's instrument panel, registers flap position in per cent of travel.

1-98. AUTOMATIC PILOT.

1-99. GENERAL.

1-100. A type MH-7 automatic pilot is provided. Automatic pilot servo motors are connected to the flight control system cables, and operate the control surfaces with surface power control on or off. The autopilot is electrically operated, requiring both direct and alternating current. Circuit breakers are on the copilot's circuit breaker panel (3, figure 1-24) and the AC circuit breaker panel (2, figure 1-24). Normal control of the automatic pilot is accomplished from a control panel (figure 1-25B) on the pilot's instrument panel.

1-101. CONTROLS.

1-102. AUTOPILOT MASTER SWITCH. This switch,

LEGEND

1. AILERON TRIM KNOB
2. TURN CONTROL KNOB
3. TRIM INDICATOR
4. ENGAGE LIGHTS
5. AUTOPILOT MASTER SWITCH

6. TRIM ACTUATOR SWITCH
7. ENGAGE SWITCH
8. ELEVATOR TRIM KNOB
9. DISENGAGED LIGHT
10. RUDDER TRIM KNOB

Figure 1-25B. Autopilot Control Panel

048087

(5, figure 1-25B) when placed in the "ON" position, applies power to the autopilot control circuits and units. When "OFF," the autopilot is turned off and disengaged.

1-103. ENGAGE SWITCH. A push-button type switch (7, figure 1-25B) is provided to engage the autopilot after the tubes and equipment have reached their normal operating temperatures and after the equipment has trimmed itself to the flight position of the airplane.

1-104. ELEVATOR, RUDDER, AND AILERON TRIM KNOBS. After the autopilot is turned on and before the engage switch is pushed, these knobs (1, 8, 10, figure 1-25B) automatically trim the autopilot to the flight position of the airplane. After the autopilot is engaged, these knobs are used as required to trim the autopilot manually. The knobs can be pushed to release the autopilot servo motors when it is desired to trim the airplane with normal trim tab controls.

1-105. TRIM ACTUATOR SWITCH. This "ON--OFF" switch (6, figure 1-25B) when placed in "ON" automatically keeps the airplane in trim to compensate for CG shifts, and prevents elevator movement as the autopilot is turned off. When the switch is "OFF," no compensating trim is provided.

1-106. AUTOPILOT RELEASE SWITCH. The pilot and copilot each have an autopilot release switch on their control wheels. The switches are provided to release all autopilot servo motors simultaneously.

1-107. TURN CONTROL KNOB. This knob (2, figure 1-25B) can be turned "RIGHT" or "LEFT" for directional control of the airplane.

1-107A. TURN CONTROL SWITCH. A "BOMBARD-IER-PILOT" turn control switch on the pilot's instrument panel, when placed in the "BOMBARDIER" position, transfers directional control of the airplane to the navigator-bombardier's station. When the switch is in the "PILOT" position, the airplane is controlled from the pilot's autopilot control panel.

1-107B. BOMBARDIER'S CONTROLLER. A bombardier's controller on the navigator's table enables the navigator to fly the airplane through coordinated turns. The turn control switch on the pilot's instrument panel must be in the "BOMBARDIER" position.

1-107C. When an "AUTOMATIC-MANUAL" switch on the bombardier's controller is in the "AUTOMATIC" position, turns are made through operation of the bombing equipment; if a turn control knob on the top of the bombardier's controller is moved out of detent, this switch will move to the "MANUAL" position. When the switch is in the "MANUAL" position, turns are made through operation of the turn control knob.

1-108. INDICATORS.

1-109. TRIM INDICATOR. When the trim actuator switch is "OFF" and the autopilot servo motors are

holding the elevators in a position out of trim, this condition will be indicated on the trim indicator (3, figure 1-25B). When the elevators are trimmed, the indicator will be zeroed.

1-110. ENGAGE LIGHTS. Two lights (4, figure 1-25B) adjacent to the engage switch, will glow when the autopilot is warmed up and ready to be engaged. The autopilot cannot be engaged until these lights are illuminated.

1-110A. DISENGAGED LIGHT. A disengaged light (9, figure 1-25B) below the engage switch is illuminated whenever the entire autopilot is disengaged. If any servo motor reaches its full travel, a limit switch will be actuated and the entire autopilot will become disengaged.

1-111. LANDING GEAR SYSTEM.

1-112. GENERAL.

1-113. On this airplane a fast acting, electrically operated landing gear is provided. This gear will retract in 11 seconds and extend in 4 seconds. Bicycle-type front and rear main landing gears are mounted on the fuselage center line and retract forward and upward into the fuselage. Lateral supporting outrigger gears are mounted under, and retract forward into, the inboard nacelles. Steering control of the front main landing gear is hydraulically accomplished by actuation of the rudder pedals. The outrigger gears are free castering up to 28 degrees inboard and 93 degrees outboard. Full swiveling of the outrigger gears for ground handling is accomplished by removing the torsion link quick disconnect pins on each outrigger gear. Two electric motors are provided for each gear. Both motors are energized for normal retraction and one for normal extension. The same motors are energized for emergency retraction through a hot wire electrical system which by-passes all safety and limit switches. Emergency extension of the landing gear is accomplished by a manually operated cable system which unlocks the gear and allows it to free fall.

1-114. CONTROLS.

1-115. LANDING GEAR CONTROL LEVERS. Interconnected "UP--OFF--DN" landing gear control levers are on the pilot's and copilot's control stands. Each control position of the pilot's lever (14, figure 1-6) is fixed by detents. The copilot's lever (18, figure 1-15) is mechanically connected with the pilot's lever. When the levers are in the "UP" position, the landing gear will retract and the brakes will be automatically applied providing the front main gear is centered and all wheels are off the ground; when in the "DN" position, the landing gear will extend; and when in the "OFF" position, the landing gear normal actuation circuits are de-energized. Landing gear control circuit breakers are on the copilot's circuit breaker panel (3, figure 1-24).

1-116. LANDING GEAR EMERGENCY RETRACTION SWITCHES. The pilot can accomplish emergency retraction of all landing gears simultaneously by lifting a single guarded switch (13, figure 1-6) on the pilot's control stand. Individual emergency retraction of any main or outrigger gear can be accomplished by holding one of four guarded switches (4, figure 1-15) on the copilot's control stand to its spring-loaded "GEAR UP" position. All landing gear emergency retraction switches will override the oleo safety switches to cause retraction of the landing gear either on the ground or in flight. Emergency landing gear retraction control circuit breakers are on the copilot's circuit breaker panel (3, figure 1-24).

1-117. LANDING GEAR EMERGENCY EXTENSION LEVER AND SELECTOR LEVERS. Emergency extension of all landing gears is largely accomplished by means of gravity forces and air drag. Unlocking of each gear in the retracted position is done by a manually operated cable system. A landing gear emergency extension lever (5, figure 1-16) and four selector levers (6, figure 1-16) are located aft and to the left of the copilot's seat. Emergency extension of each gear is accomplished by moving the corresponding selector lever to "ENGAGE" and moving the emergency extension lever fore and aft to unlock the gear. If air drag fails to lock the gear in the down position, it is possible to crank the emergency extension lever until the gear locks. Each selector lever must be returned to the "DISENGAGE" position before another selector lever is moved to "ENGAGE."

1-118. LANDING GEAR GROUND LOCKS. Accidental collapse of the forward and rear main landing gears is prevented by the insertion of shear pin type ground locks in a hole in the lower end of each main landing gear retracting screw mechanism. Accidental collapse of the outrigger gears is prevented by a strut type ground lock between a lug on the forward side of each outrigger gear strut assembly and a boss on each outrigger gear trunnion support.

1-119. INDICATORS.

1-120. LANDING GEAR INDICATING AND WARNING LIGHTS. Four green down and locked landing gear indicating lights and one red not locked landing gear warning light (15, figure 1-8) are on the pilot's instrument panel. A similar set of lights (4, figure 1-16) are provided near the landing gear emergency extension levers at the copilot's gunnery station. Four amber up and locked landing gear indicating lights and one red not locked landing gear warning light (3, figure 1-15) are on the copilot's control stand. A landing gear warning light and horn circuit breaker is on the copilot's circuit breaker panel (3, figure 1-24).

1-121. LANDING GEAR WARNING HORN. If any one of the landing gears is not down and locked when an individual throttle is retarded below minimum cruising power, a landing gear warning horn will sound. A mechanical horn release lever (20, figure 1-6) will silence the horn.

1-122. FRONT GEAR STEERING SYSTEM.

1-123. GENERAL.

1-124. The front landing gear is steerable through a hydraulic control system operated by the rudder pedals. Hydraulic pressure is supplied by the main or emergency hydraulic systems. When the landing gear is retracted, the steering control system is disconnected, hydraulic pressure is shut off, and no steering motion is transmitted to the gront gear. Centering springs center the gear during retraction. Extension of the landing gear automatically aligns the front gear with the rudder pedals after it has cleared the wheel well. The hydraulic steering units also provide for shimmy dampening.

1-125. CONTROLS.

1-126. STEERING RATIO SELECTOR LEVER. The front gear steering ratio selector lever (1, figure 1-6) on the pilot's control stand, when placed in the "TOW" position, actuates a hydraulic disconnect valve. The valve mechanically disconnects the rudder pedals from the front gear steering system. When the selector is in the "TAXI--TAKEOFF, LAND" positions, the rudder pedals are connected to the steering system in ratios best suited for these operations. "TAXI" allows a maximum wheel deflection of 60° right or left, a total of 120°, which will permit turning the airplane within a 180-foot diameter walled-in area. "TAKEOFF, LAND" position allows a maximum wheel deflection of 6° right or left, a total of 12°.

1-127. BRAKE SYSTEM.

1-128. GENERAL.

1-129. Hydraulic pressure to operate the brakes is provided by the main and emergency hydraulic systems. Brakes are on the front and rear main landing gear. Toe pressure on any one of the four rudder pedals will actuate the brakes. Should the main hydraulic system fail, emergency brakes are applied by depressing the rudder pedals farther than is normally necessary. Brakes are applied automatically when the landing gear is retracted. An anti-skid system on each wheel is available to relieve brake pressure when a skid is detected, thus forestalling tire skidding and allowing application of maximum braking.

1-130. CONTROLS.

1-131. BRAKE LOCK KNOB. Parking brakes are set by depressing the rudder pedals and pulling out a brake lock knob (38, figure 1-8) on the pilot's instrument panel.

1-132. ANTI-SKID SWITCH. An anti-skid "ON--OFF" switch (3, figure 1-11) on the pilot's switch panel controls the anti-skid system on both main landing gear wheels. Anti-skid is effective in only the main brake system. Emergency brake pressure by-passes the anti-skid valves.

048082 A

1-133. INDICATORS.

1-134. MAIN BRAKE SYSTEM PRESSURE INDICATOR. A pressure indicator (8, figure 1-20) on the copilot's hydraulic control panel is connected directly to the air side of the main system brake accumulator (figure 1-25). Main system brake pressure is not available to the brakes until the indication is greater than the minimum value.

1-135. EMERGENCY BRAKE SYSTEM PRESSURE INDICATOR. A pressure indicator (6, figure 1-20) on the copilot's hydraulic control panel is connected directly to the air side of the emergency brake accumulator (figure 1-25). Emergency brake pressure is not available to the emergency brake metering valve until the indication is greater than the minimum value.

1-136. CANOPY CONTROL SYSTEM.

1-137. GENERAL.

1-138. Hydraulic pressure is supplied from the main or emergency hydraulic system to normally open or close the canopy. In an emergency, the canopy may be jettisoned pneumatically. A lock assembly, used for positively holding the canopy in the open position during ground operation, is stowed on the walkway floor at the copilot's station.

1-139. CONTROLS.

1-40. CANOPY CONTROL LEVER. A canopy control lever (6, figure 1-13) on the right side of the pilot's station has "CLOSE--OFF--OPEN" positions. The lever is left in "OFF" except when the canopy is closed and latched hydraulically. When "OPEN", the canopy is unlatched and opened hydraulically.

1-141. CANOPY LOCK LEVER. A canopy lock pin is inserted into the latch mechanism by operation of a "LOCKED--UNLOCKED" canopy lock lever (2, figure 1-15) on the right side of the pilot's station. The lever must be in "UNLOCKED" before the canopy can be opened.

1-142. CANOPY EMERGENCY RELEASE HANDLES. Canopy emergency release handles are on the pilot's and copilot's instrument panels (37, figure 1-8 and 1, figure 1-18). Pulling out a handle unlocks and unlatches the canopy, inserts a hinge pin on the aft end of the canopy, and opens an air bottle. Pneumatic jacks lift the front of the canopy into the air stream, and it is then carried clear of the airplane. As the canopy clears the airplane, cables attached to the canopy pull out safety pins in the pilot's and copilot's seat ejection catapults, readying the latter for firing.

1-143. INDICATORS.

1-144. PNEUMATIC PRESSURE INDICATOR. A pressure indicator on the forward wall of the front wheel well indicates air pressure available for canopy jettisoning.

1-145. DRAG CHUTE SYSTEM.

1-146. GENERAL.

1-147. A 32-foot ribbon-type drag chute is installed in the aft section of the fuselage and is deployed by either the pilot or copilot by actuation of control handles at their stations. The drag chute is provided as a means of exerting large decelerating forces over the first part of the landing roll. A safety bolt in the attachment fitting will fail if the chute is opened at speeds above approximately 175 knots IAS.

1-148. CONTROLS.

1-149. DRAG CHUTE DEPLOYMENT HANDLES. Deployment handles (2A, figure 1-6 and 24, figure 1-15) to open the drag chute are above the control stand at the pilot's and copilot's stations. The handles are connected by cables to the drag chute compartment, and a pull on either handle opens the chute compartment doors and deploys the chute.

1-149A. DRAG CHUTE JETTISON HANDLES. Drag chute jettison handles (16A, figure 1-6 and 19A, figure 1-15) are on the pilot's and copilot's control stands. Pulling either one of these handles through its full travel (approximately 8 inches) jettisons the drag chute.

1-150. ASSISTED TAKE-OFF (ATO) SYSTEM.

1-151. GENERAL.

1-152. Provisions are made for installing 18 solid fuel ATO units, 9 recessed in a shroud on each side of the fuselage at the rear main wheel well. These units supply additional thrust when it is desired to shorten take-off distance. The system is electrically controlled from the ATO control panel (figure 1-9) located on the right side wall adjacent to the pilot's instrument panel. The units are fired simultaneously and, once fired, burn continuously until fuel is exhausted. In addition to the pilot's controls, an ATO safety link and a red ATO warning light are installed on the ATO control shield located in the rear main wheel well. Removal of the safety link opens the power circuit to the igniters and prevents inadvertent firing of the units. The ATO warning light, when illuminated, indicates that the ATO arming switch is in the "ARM" position. When ATO units are not installed, a flush panel may be installed in place of the ATO shroud.

1-153. CONTROLS.

1-154. ATO ARMING SWITCH. The ATO control circuit is armed through a guarded "ARM--OFF" switch (1, figure 1-9) on the ATO control panel. In the "ARM" position power is supplied to the ATO firing switch and the ATO armed warning light. When the switch is in the "OFF" position, the ATO control circuit is disarmed. Power is supplied to the ATO arming switch through a circuit breaker on the copilot's circuit breaker panel (3, figure 1-24).

U4B083 A

1-155. ATO FIRING SWITCH. With the ATO arming switch in the "ARM" position and the safety link in place, firing of the ATO units is accomplished by moving a guarded "FIRE--OFF" switch (3, figure 1-9) on the ATO control panel to the "FIRE" position. When the ATO firing switch is in the "OFF" position, the firing circuit is de-energized.

1-156. INDICATORS.

1-157. ATO ARMED INDICATOR LIGHT. A green light (2, figure 1-9) on the ATO control panel, when illuminated, indicates that the safety link is in place and the system is armed. The light will go out when the ATO firing switch is placed in the "FIRE" position or, since the light circuit is completed through a landing gear safety switch, when the airplane leaves the ground.

1-158. INSTRUMENTS.

1-159. Flight instruments are grouped in regulated alternating current, direct current, pitot-static, and miscellaneous instrument classes.

1-160. REGULATED ALTERNATING CURRENT INSTRUMENTS. Regulated alternating current instruments include gyrosyn compasses, radio compasses, and attitude gyros. Circuit breakers for the gyrosyn compasses and attitude gyros are on the AC circuit breaker panel (2, figure 1-24).

1-161. DIRECT CURRENT INSTRUMENTS. Direct current instruments include turn-and-bank and outside air temperature indicators. Circuit breakers for the turn-and-bank and outside air temperature indicators are on the copilot's circuit breaker panel (3, figure 1-24).

1-162. PITOT-STATIC INSTRUMENTS. The airspeed indicators, machmeter, altimeters, and rate-of-climb indicators are connected to pitot-static sources.

1-163. MISCELLANEOUS INSTRUMENTS. Accelerometer and magnetic compass indicators operate independently of the airplane electrical or pitot-static systems. A pilot's data indicator is used with the K-2 radar system.

1-164. INSTRUMENT PANEL VIBRATORS. Due to the low vibration level of the airplane, instrument panels are not shock mounted and vibrators are installed to induce sufficient vibration to prevent indicator pointers from sticking. A circuit breaker for the vibrators is on the copilot's circuit breaker panel (3, figure 1-24).

1-165. MISCELLANEOUS EQUIPMENT.

1-166. CREW SEATS. The pilot, copilot, and navigator are provided with ejection type seats (5, 7, 17, figure 1-2) designed for use with back type ribbon parachutes and one-man seat type life rafts. Head-

rest and seat elevation adjustment is provided on all seats. In addition, the navigator's seat can be swiveled 90° and the copilot's seat 180° to facilitate use of the navigator's table and gunner's station respectively.

1-167. DATA CASES AND CHECK LIST HOLDERS. Airplane data cases are mounted on the left sidewall at the pilot's station and on the rear pressure bulkhead at the copilot's station. In addition, a data drawer is installed under the left side of the pilot's instrument panel. A flight report holder and check list holder are mounted at the pilot's station.

1-168. ASH TRAYS. Ash trays for the crew are conveniently located.

1-169. RELIEF EQUIPMENT. Relief containers (15, figure 1-2) for the crew are stowed under the pilot's floor and are accessible from the crew passageway.

1-170. MAIN ENTRANCE LADDER. An extension type ladder (12, figure 1-2) is installed inside the main entry door to facilitate entrance into the airplane.

1-171. COVERS. Canopy, fuselage nose, pitot tube, and engine nacelle covers are stowed in the flyaway tool kit.

1-172. MOORING PROVISIONS. Demountable mooring eyes for wing fittings are stowed in the flyaway tool kit.

1-173. FLYAWAY TOOL KIT. A flyaway tool kit is stowed in the bomb bay.

1-173A. RAIN REPELLENT KIT. A kit for applying a rain repellent coating to the windshield is stowed in the unpressurized section above the entrance door.

1-174. EMERGENCY EQUIPMENT.

1-175. SAFETY BELTS AND SHOULDER HARNESSES. All crew seats are provided with both safety belts and shoulder harnesses.

1-176. SHOULDER HARNESS INERTIA REEL LOCK HANDLE. A handle with "LOCKED" and "RELEASED" positions is located on the left side of each crew member's seat. A latch is provided for positively retaining the handle at either position of the quadrant. By pressing down on the top of the handle the latch is released and the handle may then be moved freely from one position to the other. When the handle is in the "RELEASED" position, the reel harness cable will extend to allow the crew member to lean forward; however, the reel harness cable will automatically lock when an impact force of 2 to 3 g's is encountered. When the reel is locked in this manner, it will remain locked until the handle is moved to the "LOCKED" position and then returned to the "RELEASED" position. When the handle is in the "LOCKED" position, the reel harness cable is manually locked so that the crew member is pre-

048084 A

vented from bending forward. The "LOCKED" position is used only when a crash landing is anticipated. This position provides an added safety precaution over and above that of the automatic safety lock.

1-177. EJECTION SEAT MECHANISM. Each crew member's seat is equipped with a seat ejection catapult for ejecting seat and occupant during bailout. Elevation adjustment is made possible by actuation of a lever (10, figure 1-26) on the left side of each seat. Raising the lever pulls keeper pins out of the seat frame, disconnecting the seat from the catapult and permitting the seat to be raised or lowered. When the lever is returned to the normal position, spring pressure assists in seating and retaining the pins in the holes selected. Rotation of the navigator's seat is made possible by raising a rotation latch release lever located under the front edge of the seat. Rotation of the copilot's seat is made possible by pressing a button in the end of a rotation control lever, located on the right side of the seat, and raising the lever. This action releases the seat for rotation and tilts it to the vertical position in order to clear the airplane structure during rotation.

1-177A. A safety pin in each seat ejection catapult prevents its firing until the canopy or emergency hatch, through which the seat ejects, is clear of the airplane. Once the canopy or hatch has cleared the airplane, seat jection is accomplished through a firing lever (4, figure 1-26) stowed in each right armrest. Turning a knob on the end of the lever in a counterclockwise direction causes spring pressure to extend the lever, extend footrests, and lock the shoulder harness inertia reel. Raising the firing lever will then fire the catapult. As the seat leaves the airplane, interphone, and oxygen, and suit heater lines are automatically severed at a disconnect mounted on the seat. A ground lock assembly (3, 5, 7, figure 1-26) consisting of a red streamer with

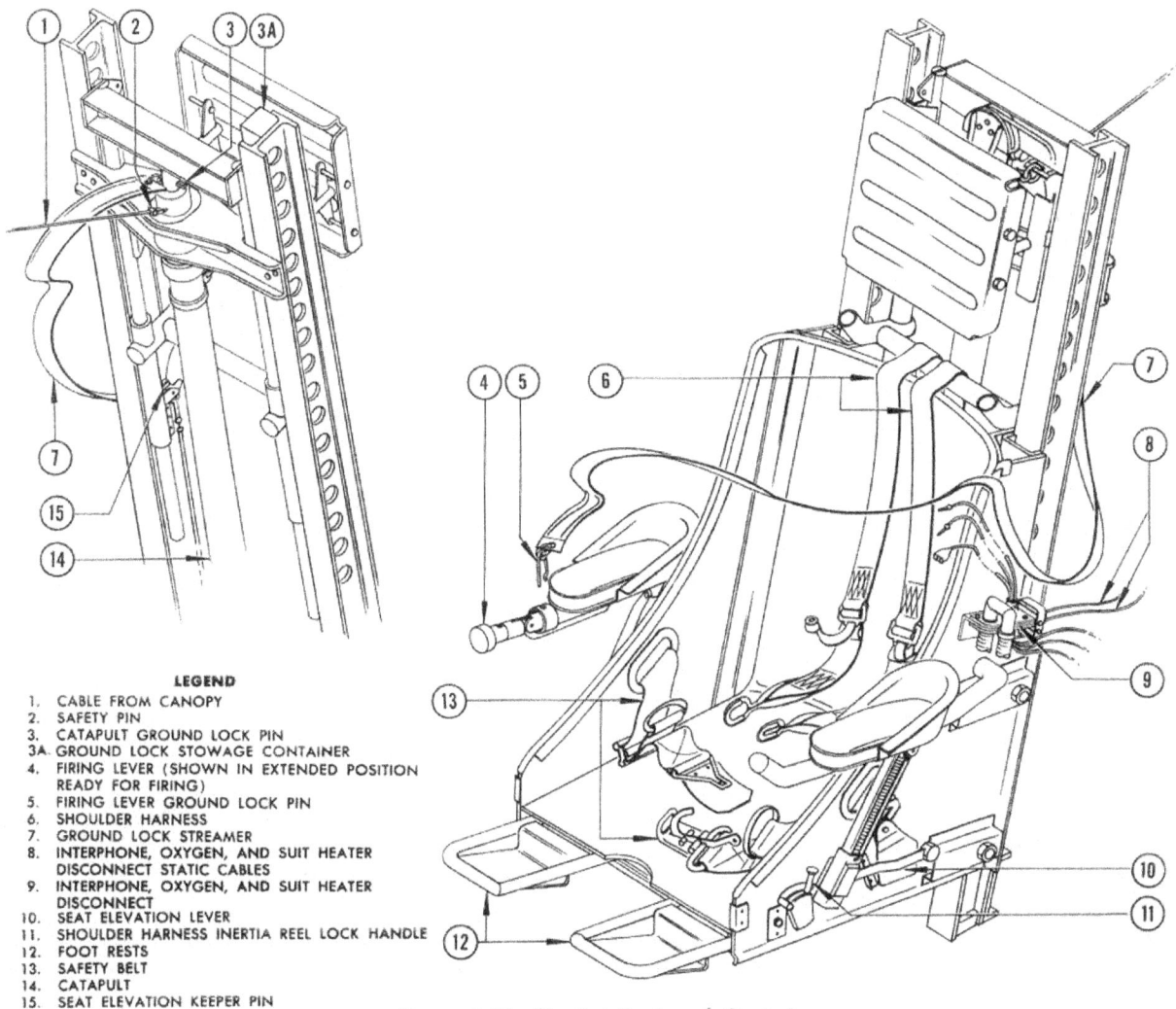

LEGEND

1. CABLE FROM CANOPY
2. SAFETY PIN
3. CATAPULT GROUND LOCK PIN
3A. GROUND LOCK STOWAGE CONTAINER
4. FIRING LEVER (SHOWN IN EXTENDED POSITION READY FOR FIRING)
5. FIRING LEVER GROUND LOCK PIN
6. SHOULDER HARNESS
7. GROUND LOCK STREAMER
8. INTERPHONE, OXYGEN, AND SUIT HEATER DISCONNECT STATIC CABLES
9. INTERPHONE, OXYGEN, AND SUIT HEATER DISCONNECT
10. SEAT ELEVATION LEVER
11. SHOULDER HARNESS INERTIA REEL LOCK HANDLE
12. FOOT RESTS
13. SAFETY BELT
14. CATAPULT
15. SEAT ELEVATION KEEPER PIN

Figure 1-26. Ejection Seat and Controls

048050A

locking pins at each end is used to prevent operation of the firing lever and firing of the catapult while on the ground. One pin is inserted through the firing lever and armrest; the other pin is inserted in the catapult shipping pin hole. Both pins must be removed before take-off and the ground lock assembly stowed in a container provided on the back of each seat headrest. Safety latches on the navigator's and copilot's seats prevent extension of the firing levers when the seats are not in the forward position.

1-178. NAVIGATOR'S EMERGENCY ESCAPE HATCH. An emergency escape hatch (figure 3-2) is installed above the navigator's seat ahead of the pilot's windshield. An emergency hatch release lever is located just outboard of the forward left corner of the hatch. Moving this lever inboard releases the latching dogs holding the hatch and permits a spring-loaded actuator to force the leading edge of the hatch into the air stream. As the hatch clears the airplane, a cable attached to the hatch pulls out a safety pin in the navigator's seat ejection catapult, readying the latter for firing. External means for releasing the hatch is provided by a pull handle which is accessible through a small hinged door in the left side fuselage skin outboard of the hatch. Pulling this handle releases the hatch in the same manner as does the navigator's hatch release lever.

1-179. FIRE FIGHTING EQUIPMENT. A hand operated carbon tetrachloride fire extinguisher (2, figure 3-1) is mounted on the pilot's floor immediately aft of the navigator's seat. No fixed fire extinguishing system is installed.

WARNING

When using a carbon tetrachloride fire extinguisher, only the minimum quantity necessary should be applied at the base of the fire. Exposure to smoke and fumes must be avoided. The fluid is poisonous and the fumes are extremely toxic. The area should be ventilated as soon as possible after fire is extinguished.

1-180. EMERGENCY ALARM. An emergency alarm bell (3, figure 3-1) is located in the walkway imme-

diately aft of the navigator's seat. A guarded "ON--OFF" switch (1, figure 1-11) on the pilot's switch panel controls the bell. In the "ON" position power is supplied directly from the battery to ring the bell. In the "OFF" position the circuit is de-energized.

1-181. FIRST AID KITS. Aeronautic first aid kits (1, figure 3-1) are mounted in the walkway opposite the copilot's seat and on the right side wall at the navigator's station.

1-182. HAND AXE. A small hand axe (4, figure 3-1) is mounted in the walkway opposite the pilot's seat.

1-183. FIRE WARNING SYSTEM. Thermally actuated switch type fire detector units are mounted in the accessory section, air guide section, and tail cone section of each engine nacelle. Six fire warning lights (9, figure 1-8), one for each engine, are on the pilot's instrument panel. When any one fire detector unit is actuated, the warning light for the affected engine is illuminated. Two fire warning circuit continuity "TEST--NORMAL" switches (1, 2, figure 1-10), the left switch for engines 1, 2, and 3 and the right switch for engines 4, 5, and 6, are on the fire warning test panel. When the switches are in the "TEST" position, illumination of the warning lights indicates that the warning circuit continuity is satisfactory. In the "NORMAL" position, the circuit is armed for fire warning and, as a safety factor in the event of an open circuit or wire breakage, an additional circuit for each engine is connected to the fire detector units through the switches. A circuit breaker for the fire warning lights is on the copilot's circuit breaker panel (3, figure 1-24).

1-184. OPERATIONAL EQUIPMENT.

1-185. The following equipment and its operation is described in section IV, "Operational Equipment":
 Cabin Heating, Ventilating, and Pressurizing
   Systems
 Anti-icing Systems
 Communications and Associated Electronic
   Equipment
 Lighting Equipment
 Oxygen System
 Navigation Equipment
 Gunnery Equipment
 Photographic Equipment
 Bombing Equipment

048085 A

SECTION II NORMAL OPERATING INSTRUCTIONS

2-1. BEFORE ENTERING AIRPLANE.

2-2. RESTRICTIONS.

a. See figure A-2 for limits other than those listed below.

b. Maximum IAS for raising landing gear - 218 knots.

c. Maximum IAS for half wing flaps - 218 knots.

d. Drag chute operation - deploy only after touch-down.

e. Maximum IAS for bomb doors open - no restriction

f. Maximum IAS for opening canopy - 215 knots,

g. Maximum forward CG in flight - 12% MAC.

h. Maximum aft CG in flight - 33% MAC.

i. Maximum forward CG for take-off or landing - 14% MAC.

j. Maximum aft CG for take-off or landing - 35% MAC.

k. Maximum take-off gross weight - 162,500 pounds.

l. All acrobatics are prohibited.

m. For maximum air speed and Mach number limitations, see the charts in Appendix I.

These limitations and restrictions are subject to change and the latest service directives and orders must be consulted.

2-3. TAKE-OFF WEIGHT AND BALANCE. Check the take-off and anticipated landing weights and balances with the "Handbook of Weight and Balance," AN 01-1B-40.

2-4. EXTERIOR INSPECTION. Check the following items before entering the airplane:

a. Check Forms 1 and F for status of airplane and obtain ground crew report including fuel, oil, and oxygen quantities. Establish that nozzles installed in the empennage combustion heaters are suitable for the fuel with which the airplane has been serviced.

b. Condition of tires.

c. Oleo strut extension.

d. Canopy jettison air battle pressure at 2000 PSI.

e. Landing gear ground safety locks, bomb bay door safety locks, air intake plugs, and pitot covers removed, check air intakes for foreign matter.

f. Outrigger gear torsion link pins in place.

g. Wheel chocks in place.

h. Access openings and fairing secure.

i. Control surfaces.

j. Frost, ice, snow, or dust removed from wing and empennage surfaces.

k. Portable fire extinguishers and external power source available.

l. ATO safety links removed.

CAUTION

Remain clear of ATO firing area during inspection.

m. Drag chute installed.

n. Flaperon accumulator air pressure at least 500 PSI.

o. Hydraulic fluid quantity on sight gage in front wheel well.

p. Wing slats and flaps full extended.

q. Check ground crew on interphone.

2-5. MINIMUM CREW REQUIREMENTS. The minimum crew requirements for this airplane are a pilot and copilot. Additional crew members as required to accomplish special missions will be added at the discretion of the Commanding Officer.

2-6. ENTERING THE AIRPLANE.

2-7. Entrance into the airplane is gained through a door in the lower left side of the fuselage immediately aft of the radome.

2-8. INTERIOR INSPECTION (ALL FLIGHTS). Check the following items on entering the airplane:

a. Entrance door and pressure door closed and latched.

b. Parachutes and other personal equipment available.

c. Ejection seat canopy cable safety pin in place.

d. Ejection seat keeper pin in place.

e. Ejection seat firing lever retracted.

f. Pull streamer pins.

g. Check interphone and oxygen disconnect secure.

h. Oxygen bail-out bottle charged; static line connected; and safety pin removed.

i. Navigator's emergency escape hatch closed and latched.

j. Landing gear emergency extension selector levers "DISENGAGE."

k. Canopy lock assembly removed and stowed.

2-8A. INTERIOR INSPECTION (NIGHT FLIGHTS). Check all lighting equipment and have flashlights available prior to all night flights.

048053A

2-9. FUEL SYSTEM MANAGEMENT.

2-10. BEFORE STARTING ENGINES. Set up fuel system controls for starting as follows:

a. No. 2 engine fuel selector switch "Tank-to-Engine and Manifold."

b. All other fuel selector switches "Tank-to-Engine."

c. Check fuel boost pressure warning lights illuminated.

d. Check that fuel quantity indicators read full; depress fuel quantity indicator test switches.

NOTE

The fuel quantity indicators are calibrated for a level flight attitude except that the full mark is calibrated for a taxi attitude. The indicators will read low when the airplane is on the ground for all quantities less than full.

e. Auxiliary tank valve and boost pump switches "OFF."

2-11. DURING FLIGHT. The fuel consumption and transfer procedure during flight is as follows:

a. Use fuel equally from the three main tanks by retaining the No. 2 engine fuel selector switch on "Tank-to-Engine and Manifold" and all other fuel selector switches on "Tank-to-Engine."

b. Transfer fuel from auxiliary to main tanks in accordance with the charts in the "Handbook of Weight and Balance," AN 01-1B-40. Accomplish transfer by positioning auxiliary tank valve and boost pump switches "ON"; transfer pressure is indicated by a "P" tab in the auxiliary tank pressure indicator.

c. After fuel transfer, equalize main tank fuel levels by positioning fuel selector switches for high level tank to "Tank-to-Manifold and Engine"; fuel selector switches for low level tank on "Manifold-to-Engine"; and checking fuel pressures within limits.

2-12. BEFORE LANDING. Accomplish before landing fuel system check as follows:

a. No. 2 fuel selector switch "Tank-to-Engine and Manifold"; all other fuel selector switches "Tank-to-Engine."

NOTE

In the event of minimum fuel quantities, position the fuel selector switches for all engines to "Tank-to-Engine and Manifold."

b. Fuel pressures within limits.

c. Fuel boost pressure warning lights not illuminated.

2-13. ALTERNATE FUEL GRADE OPERATING LIMITS.

2-14. The operating limits are identical for the recommended and alternate fuel grades.

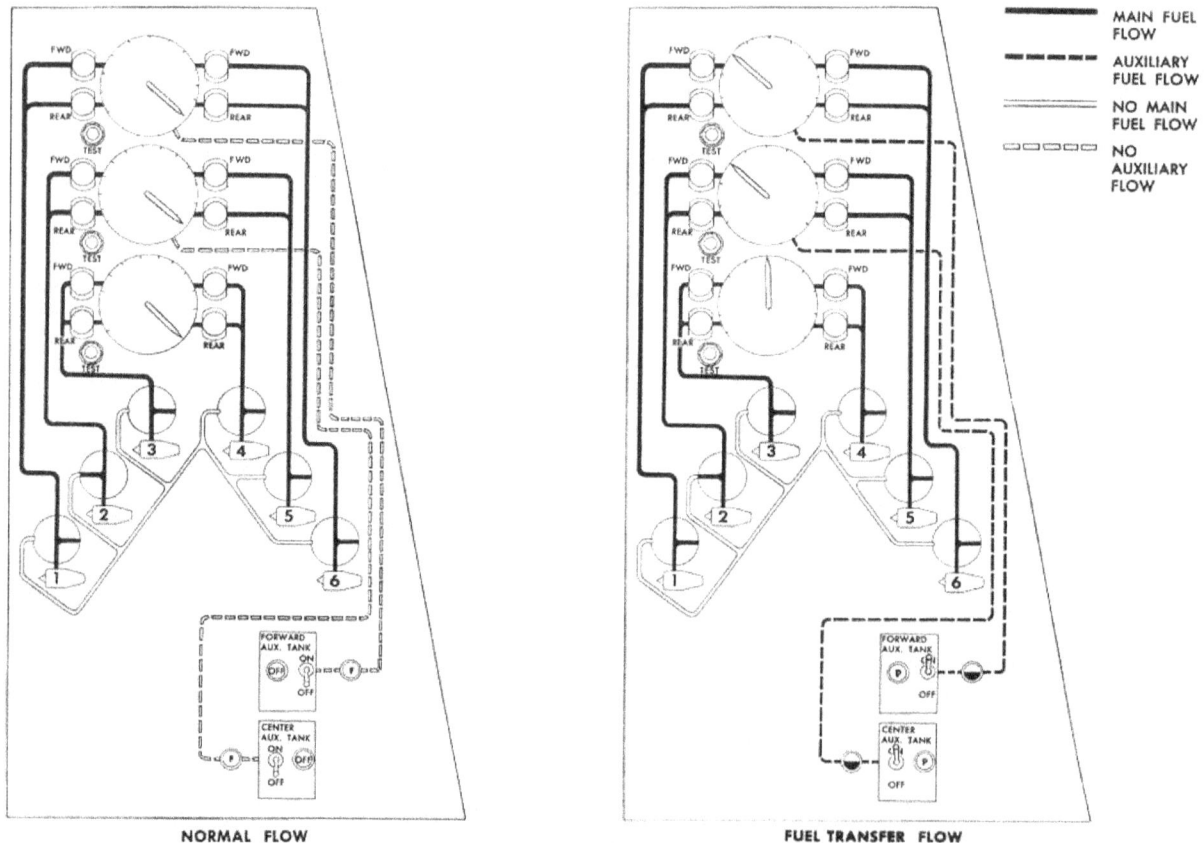

Figure 2-1. Fuel System Management

2-15. BEFORE STARTING ENGINES.

PILOT

1. Check and adjust seat belt, shoulder harness, mike cord, oxygen equipment, rudder pedals, and seat

2. Check oxygen

3. Battery switch "OFF"

4. Landing gear control lever and emergency switches "OFF"

5. Wing flap lever "OFF"

6. ATO arming and firing switches "OFF"

7. Surface power control switches "OFF"

8. Wing and empennage anti-icing control switches "OFF"

9. Bomb salvo switch and bomb door switch off

10. Throttles "CUTOFF"

11. Battery switch "ON"; notify copilot to check battery; when battery is checked, turn battery switch "OFF"

12. Have external power connected

13. Directional damper switch "ON"

14. Heat selector switch "AUTO"; cabin temperature selector rheostat as desired

15. Autopilot master switch "ON"

COPILOT

1. Adjust seat belt, shoulder harness, mike cord, oxygen equipment, rudder pedals, and seat; lock seat swivel

2. Check oxygen

3. Inverter switches "OFF" for battery check

4. Landing gear control lever and emergency switches "OFF"

5. Wing flap lever and emergency wing flap switches "OFF"

10. Unregulated AC power switch "EXT POWER"

11. When pilot turns battery switch "ON," check battery voltage on the DC bus

12. Notify pilot when external power is connected

13. All circuit breakers pushed in

14. Check generator switches "ON"

15. Check push-to-test lights

16. Check inverter voltages on the main, spare, and secondary inverters; leave switches in "MAIN INVERTER" and "SECONDARY INVERTER"

17. Check inverter automatic change-over by turning off main inverter circuit breaker; return main inverter to the main bus by turning main inverter switch "OFF" before resetting the main inverter circuit breaker; allow 15 to 20 seconds to elapse before returning the main inverter switch to "MAIN INVERTER"

NOTE

The spare inverter will take up the load of either the main or secondary bus in the event of a main or secondary inverter failure; it will take up the main bus load if both main and secondary inverters fail; a check for double failure can be made but is not deemed necessary

0480340A

─────────── 2-15. BEFORE STARTING ENGINES (CONTINUED). ───────────

PILOT

COPILOT

18. Windshield and pitot heat switches "OFF"

19. Test emergency alarm

20. Antiskid switch "ON"

21. Master air conditioning switch "ON"

22. Cabin air selector switch "COMPR;

NOTE

For hot weather, the ground blower can be operated by positioning this switch to "RAM"

23. Cabin pressure regulation selector switch as desired

24. Canopy defrost switch "OFF"

NOTE

Additional ventilation can be obtained by turning this switch "ON"

25. Wing slat warning horn switch "NORMAL"

26. Fire warning test switches "TEST"; check fire warning lights; then release test switches to "NORMAL"

27. Check push-to-test lights

28. Surface lock lever "UNLOCK"

28. Check normal and emergency operation of wing flaps and slats; leave wing flap lever "OFF"

CAUTION

Avoid striking flap up or down limits on the emergency system by completing travel with the normal system

29. Steering ratio selector lever "TOW"

29. Main hydraulic system charging valve switch "PRESSURIZE"

30. Ignition switches "NORMAL"

30. Emergency hydraulic pump switch "OFF"

31. Emergency cabin pressure release handle in place; depress heat reset button

31. Request permission from pilot to bleed down emergency and main hydraulic systems by operating brakes; check warning lights and accumulator pressures

32. Surface power control switches "ON"

32. Check emergency hydraulic pump operation by positioning switch to "ON" and "AUTO"; leave switch in "AUTO"

33. With surface power control on, check controls for free and correct movement, check flaperon action, and check trim tabs for free movement

33. Check emergency hydraulic warning lights not illuminated

34. Surface power control switches "OFF"

35. With surface power control off, check controls for free and correct movement

36. Zero trim tabs

37. Set parking brakes when notified by copilot

0480540A

2-15. BEFORE STARTING ENGINES (CONTINUED).

PILOT

COPILOT

38. Check VHF radio and radio compass

39. Check altimeter and other instrument settings

39. Check altimeter and other instruments

40. Check proper functioning and sense of autopilot trim knobs and turn control knob; check action of autopilot release switch on control wheel; place turn control switch in "BOMBARDIER" position and have navigator check his turn controller

40. Check action of autopilot release switch on control wheel

NOTE

On airplanes in which the K-2 radar system is incomplete or inoperative, the bombardier's controller switch is lockwired in the "MANUAL" position

41. Check bomb bay doors clear; bomb door switch "CLOSE"

41. Zero trim tabs

42. Accomplish before starting engines fuel system management check

43. Have ATO link installed

44. Check parking brakes set

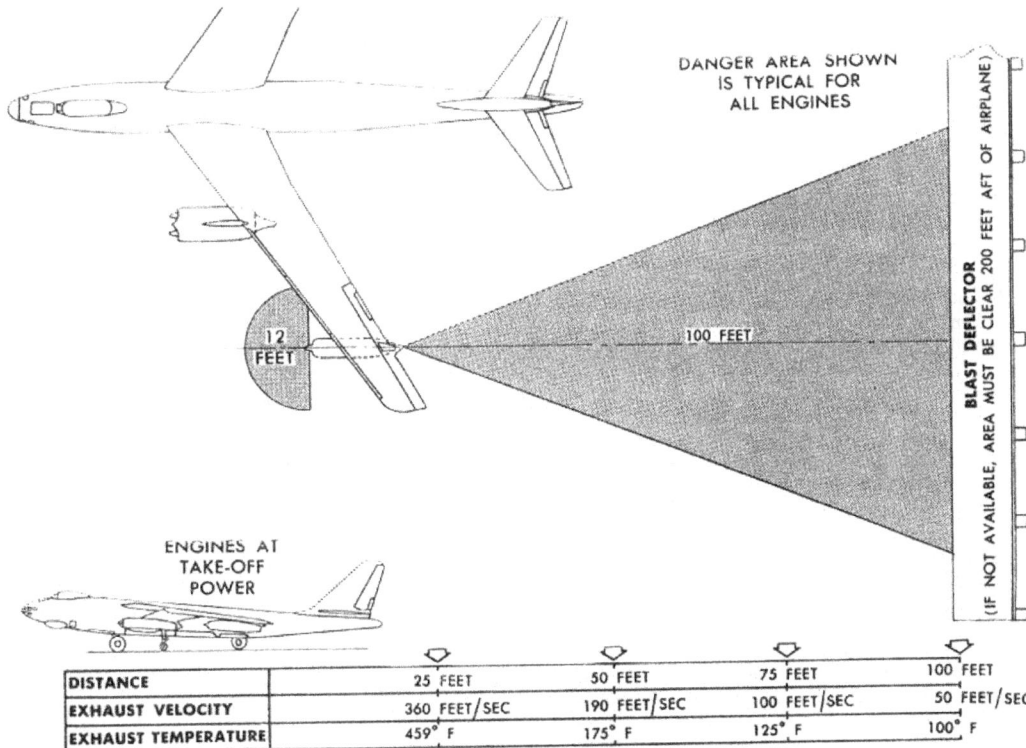

DANGER AREA SHOWN IS TYPICAL FOR ALL ENGINES

100 FEET

12 FEET

BLAST DEFLECTOR (IF NOT AVAILABLE, AREA MUST BE CLEAR 200 FEET AFT OF AIRPLANE)

ENGINES AT TAKE-OFF POWER

DISTANCE	25 FEET	50 FEET	75 FEET	100 FEET
EXHAUST VELOCITY	360 FEET/SEC	190 FEET/SEC	100 FEET/SEC	50 FEET/SEC
EXHAUST TEMPERATURE	459° F	175° F	125° F	100° F

Figure 2-2. Danger Areas

——————————— 2-16. STARTING ENGINES. ———————————

PILOT

COPILOT

WARNING

Prior to starting engine and during engine operation, be sure that danger areas around air intake ducts and exhaust jet nozzles are clear of personnel, aircraft, and vehicles; air intake suction is sufficient to kill or seriously injure personnel if drawn into or suddenly against the air intake; danger in rear of exhaust jet is created by high exhaust temperature and velocity

1. Check ground crew ready to notify pilot when engine starts and engine danger areas clear (figure 2-2)

1. Move DC voltmeter selector switch to engine to be started

CAUTION

Whenever practicable start and run up engine with aircraft on clean concrete or other paved surface to minimize possibility of dirt or other objects being drawn into engine compressor and damaging engine

2. Starter switch "START"; then release switch (engine starting sequence 4, 5, 6, 3, 2, and 1)

2. Inform pilot when 6 to 7% RPM has been reached.

3. When engine speed has reached 6 to 7% RPM rapidly open throttle to but not beyond the "IDLE" stop; as the fuel pressure reaches 20 to 35 PSI, ignition should occur (as evidenced by an increase in exhaust temperature); retard throttle immediately and manipulate carefully to control exhaust gas temperature at 700° C; the engine should fire at or before 9% RPM

3. When first inboard engine is started, check that the hydraulic pump pressure warning light goes out and that the main hydraulic system pressure builds up; when the second inboard engine is being started, check that the remaining hydraulic pump ressure warning light goes out

NOTE

If ignition does not occur by the time the engine has reached 9% RPM, or within 15 seconds after opening the throttle, close the throttle and momentarily position the starter switch to "CUTOFF"; allow at least 3 minutes for complete fuel drainage before attempting another start; the starter should not be used to turn the engine longer than 1 minute without the assistance of combustion; starter is limited to three runs of 1 minute duration during any 30-minute period; discontinue start if ignition is not on as soon as the throttle has been advanced.

CAUTION

Never turn ignition on after throttle has been advanced

048055uA

─── 2-16. STARTING ENGINES (CONTINUED). ───

PILOT

4. After starting, when the exhaust gas temperature has stabilized, advance the throttle carefully to increase RPM to 28 to 35% keeping the exhaust temperature at approximately 700° C; if starter cutoff does not occur, momentarily position starter switch to "CUTOFF"

NOTE

The time required to accelerate to idle RPM varies from about 1 minute for cool days to about 2 minutes on hot days

CAUTION

Any one start or acceleration during which the exhaust temperature exceeds 980° C momentarily, or any five starts or accelerations during which the exhaust temperature exceeds 870° C momentarily, shall constitute overtemperature operation and requires that the engine be carefully inspected before flight (the five hot starts constitute an inspection requirement regardless of the time elapsed between the starts); the temperature and duration of all overtemperature operation (870° C) shall be entered on the Form 1; engine overspeed operation exceeding 104% RPM, either with or without overtemperature, requires an engine overhaul

5. Stabilize engine at 35% RPM and check all engine instruments before accelerating to a higher RPM

6. Check for positive oil pressure rise

7. Start remaining engines as above

COPILOT

4. Check for starter cutoff at approximately 25% RPM by observing a voltage drop to zero on voltmeter; if starter cutoff does not occur, notify pilot

048035 bA

2-17. BEFORE TAXIING.

PILOT

1. Battery switch "ON"
2. Have external power disconnected
3. Surface power control switches "ON"

5. Check flight controls for free and correct movement
6. Close and lock canopy

7. Have chocks removed
8. Release parking brakes
9. Steering ratio selector lever "TAXI"

COPILOT

1. Check hydraulic pressure and fluid quantity

3. Check generator switches "ON" and generators charging
4. Alternator switches "ON"
5. Unregulated AC power switch "MAIN"

6. Check canopy latched and locking pins in place

2-18. TAXI INSTRUCTIONS.

2-19. All steering during taxiing is accomplished by use of the front gear steering system. Differential braking is not possible with the bicycle type landing gear and differential thrusts on the engines should not be used because this method is ineffective. Taxi the airplane with engines operating at 35% RPM or more as needed. Use the brakes as little as possible.

NOTE

The high fuel consumption (approximately 100 to 150 pounds per minute) during taxiing makes it necessary to hold engine speed and taxi time to an absolute minimum.

2-20. BEFORE TAKE-OFF.

PILOT

1. Close and lock canopy (if opened for taxiing)

2. Steering ratio selector lever "TAKE-OFF, LAND"

3. Check wing flaps full down

4. Check surface power control switches "ON"

5. Check trim tabs zeroed

6. Check fuel control panel for inoperative boost pumps indicated by red warning lights

7. Fight copilot on elevator and aileron controls

8. Arm rests down

9. ATO arming switch "ARM"; check warning light illuminated

COPILOT

1. Check canopy latched and locking pins in place

2. Engage and adjust control column

3. Check wing flaps full down

4. Check hydraulic pressure and fluid quantity

5. Check trim tabs zeroed

7. Fight pilot on elevator and aileron controls

8. Arm rests down

2-21. TAKE-OFF INSTRUCTIONS.

2-22. GENERAL. Close attention should be given to the correct take-off procedure on this airplane because differences from reciprocating engine bombers appreciably affect ground roll. The principal new factors are jet engine thrust which is constant throughout take-off, the bicycle type landing gear which fixes the take-off angle of attack, and the ATO units which shorten take-off distances. It should be realized that take-off distances can be accurately estimated, particularly because the factor of pilot technique on the elevator control is fixed by the bicycle type landing gear. To estimate take-off distance, the pilot should ascertain the following data and apply it:
a. Gross weight.
b. Ground temperature.
c. Field elevation.
d. Wind direction and velocity.
e. Tail pipe temperature (estimate and check on engine run-up).

2-22A. TAKE-OFF THRUST. On this airplane all take-offs are to be made at 100% RPM. Thrust at this setting varies with exhaust gas temperature, outside air temperature, and field pressure altitude. The thrust available for take-off is limited by the stabilized exhaust temperature limits as shown in figure 2-2A. The stabilized exhaust gas temperature that will result from a 100% RPM take-off can be controlled by varying the nozzle area through the in-

stallation of area reducing tabs. Although the installation of these tabs is a ground crew function, the pilot should be familiar with the calculations necessary to arrive at the proper tab area. These calculations are given in appendix I (see paragraph A-1).

2-22B. From the information in appendix I it is also possible to compute the per cent of standard rated sea level thrust that is available for any setting of stabilized exhaust gas temperature (see paragraph A-3).

2-23. NORMAL TECHNIQUE. Minimum take-off distance is attained by maintaining military rated RPM throughout the take-off run with the flaps fully extended. To preclude any possibility of stalling and to obtain optimum control and climb after take-off, allow the airplane to fly off the ground with both gears leaving simultaneously. The elevators may be used to pull the front gear off when the airplane appears to rock between the front and rear gears.

2-24. ATO TECHNIQUE. The ATO is used to shorten take-off distance and provide additional ATO thrust as a safety factor for take-off. The optimum time to fire the ATO units is 10 seconds before take-off. The technique is to maintain the initial climb IAS and gain additional altitude as soon as possible. The thrust period after firing ATO is 14 seconds. The airplane climb angle should be decreased slightly before termination of ATO thrust to prevent excessive loss of IAS.

--- 2-25. TAKE-OFF. ---

PILOT

1. Apply brakes
2. Throttles "OPEN"
3. Release brakes
4. 10 seconds before take-off, ATO firing switch "FIRE"
5. Signal copilot to raise landing gear

6. Signal copilot to raise wing flaps

COPILOT

2. Check full RPM; generator voltage and load; and alternator voltage

5. On signal from pilot, landing gear control lever "UP" (retraction time 11 seconds); notify pilot when the four up and locked lights come on

CAUTION

If landing gear retraction is discontinued for any reason, position the landing gear control lever to "OFF" for a few seconds and then reposition to "UP"

6. On signal from pilot, wing flap lever "UP"; notify pilot when flaps are up

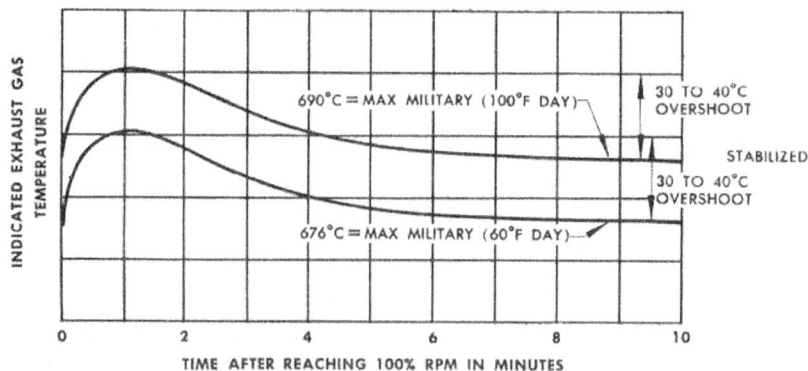

Figure 2-2A. Exhaust Gas Temperature Stabilization

NOTE

EXHAUST GAS TEMPERATURE DOES NOT STABILIZE FOR SOME TIME AFTER 100% RPM IS REACHED. THE TEMPERATURE OVERSHOOTS DURING TAKE-OFF AND REQUIRES SEVERAL MINUTES TO STABILIZE AT CONSTANT VALUE. THIS SURGE DOES NOT APPRECIABLY AFFECT THE THRUST. THE TEMPER-ATURE SHOULD NEVER EXCEED 690°C EXCEPT AS SHOWN ABOVE OR DURING ENGINE ACCELERATION.

2-26. CLIMB.

2-27. The best IAS to climb is about 360 knots at sea level. This speed should be reduced approximately 3 knots for each 1000 feet gain in altitude.

2-28. FLIGHT CHARACTERISTICS.

2-29. GENERAL. Flight characteristics of the air-plane are normal for its size except for the differ-ences common to jet airplanes and for the lighter control forces necessary. The lack of propeller slipstream over the wing results in almost identical. power-on and power-off stalling speeds. The lack of propeller drag results in slower deceleration of the jet airplane in the power-off condition.

2-30. SURFACE POWER CONTROL CHARACTER-ISTICS. Under normal conditions, all flight control movement is accomplished through the surface power control system. Hydraulic pressure is used to re-duce the control forces required, and consequently, the flying characteristics of this airplane are greatly improved over former bomber type airplanes to a point where fighter airplane flying characteristics are are approached.

2-31. RANGE. Maximum range is obtained by climbing to performance altitude as rapidly as poss-ible and then maintaining .74 Mach throughout the cruise portion of the flight, slowly increasing alti-tude, about 1500 feet per hour, as fuel is consumed. Although .74 Mach is optimum, the airplane can be flown at .70 to .76 Mach with a maximum loss in range of only 3%. Cruising at Mach numbers above or below these values will result in an appreciable loss in range. A good rule to follow is never to fly below .74 Mach for six-engine operation. It should be kept in mind that, when JP-3 or gasoline is the fuel, a loss in range of up to 20% can occur due to fuel boiling. This boiling takes place when the fuel

is hot at take-off and a rapid climb is made to alti-tude which does not allow time for the fuel to cool. An additional loss of range can be caused by ex-cessive air bleed from the compressors. This loss is less than 1% during flight and less than 3% for take-off.

2-32. A Machmeter has been provided for use when flying at high Mach numbers. It is advisable to occasionally check the accuracy of the Machmeter by means of the airspeed indicator and altimeter, using the Mach number conversion chart in Appendix I.

2-33. BUFFETING. Buffeting is the term used to describe the aerodynamic effects on the airplane due to flow separation over the airfoils. This separation can occur under the following flight conditions:
a. Low indicated air speeds (stall range).
b. Accelerated flight (positive "g" acceleration).
c. High speed or Mach number effect.

2-34. The spread between low and high speed buffet-ing varies with altitude, with the maximum spread occuring at sea level. The spread is continually de-creasing as altitude is gained until the low and high buffeting speeds become the same. This means that the indicated stalling speed increases with altitude. It is also a function of airplane gross weight. For example, at a gross weight of 130,000 pounds and an altitude of 40,000 feet, the spread between the low and high speed buffeting is 70 knots. Under these conditions, assuming a cruising speed of .79 Mach, buffeting will occur at a positive acceleration of 1.2 g's. See the Appendix curves for complete buffeting data.

2-35. Initial high speed buffeting is noted by a very slight shaking of the airplane which increases in magnitude as the speed or acceleration is increased. Buffeting due to acceleration may also be encountered in turns at high altitudes. No rolling moments are encountered during buffeting; however, pitch-up is present during both high speed and acceleration buffeting. Operation near the buffeting range at high altitudes must be conducted with caution because of the following:

a. Decrements in air speed are difficult to accomplish at altitude due to the high minimum obtainable RPM (approximately 90% at 40,000 feet).

b. A very slight nose-down attitude with all engines at minimum RPM can result in increasing air speed.

c. Accelerations of 1.1 to 1.2 g's at high altitudes will promote considerable buffeting. Because of this condition, it is necessary to appreciably increase the drag or decrease the thrust. Extending the landing gear is recommended to increase the drag while, under emergency conditions, cutting two or more (depending on conditions) engines is recommended to decrease the thrust.

NOTE

Do not attempt to restart the engines at extreme altitudes; refer to engine air-starting procedure in section III.

2-36. Recovery from the buffeting range in level flight may be accomplished by reducing power to the minimum obtainable engine RPM and waiting for the airplane to decelerate.

2-37. HIGH SPEEDS. Due to the lateral control restrictions, the airplane is restricted to 455 knots IAS. The aerodynamic characteristics restrict the maximum allowable indicated Mach number to .85. The airplane has been satisfactorily flown at this Mach number at an altitude of 30,000 feet and a gross weight of 110,000 pounds. However, it is mandatory that the pilot be aware that the Mach number at which high speed buffeting occurs is a function of altitude and gross weight. Consequently, the Mach number where high speed buffeting is encountered will vary, on different flights and/or long missions, with gross weight and altitude changes.

2-38. WING FLAP OPERATION IN FLIGHT.

2-39. Wing flaps are necessary on this airplane to obtain maximum margins of safety over the stalling speed. The flaps are designed to provide maximum lift with minimum drag, and should not be operated with all the variations used on other airplanes. Flaps should be fully extended during all low speed flight. The following procedures should be used:

a. Take-off. Flaps fully extended to obtain sufficient angle of attack and shorten ground roll. Flaperon control will operate only with flaps full down.

b. Climb. Start flap retraction 20 knots above take-off speed with airplane in a slight climb. The flaps retract slowly (approximately 40 seconds) to match airplane acceleration and to avoid necessity of milking the flaps. At high gross weights, acceleration and climb after take-off should be made so flaps are completely retracted just as 218 knots IAS is reached.

c. Approach. Flaps fully extended when indicated air speed is decreased to 175 knots. There is no advantage to partial extension, since flaps have low drag. Extension is rapid to avoid stalling if airplane is decelerating rapidly.

2-40. STALLS.

2-41. The stall characteristics of the airplane are very satisfactory. Providing the following procedure is adhered to, no difficulty will be encountered in the execution of practice stalls:

a. As a safety measure, an altitude of 20,000 feet should be used.

b. Use the minimum obtainable RPM (for the stall altitude) and the minimum rate of approach to the stall (approximately 1 knot per second). This procedure will result in a moderate climb angle of approximately 10 degrees which will eliminate the severe buffeting that occurs at steep stall entry angles.

NOTE

Engine RPM has no effect on stall characteristics, or speeds.

c. Stall warning is adequate and will occur from 8 to 12 knots prior to the stall, depending on the approach rate. Initial stall warning appears in the form of a "nibble" increasing progressively to moderate buffeting at the stall. This buffeting is in the form of a vertical bounce of moderate magnitude and a low (approximately four cycles per second) frequency.

d. Just prior to the complete stall, a very slight pitch-up of from 2 to 4 degrees will occur. This pitch-up is not of sufficient magnitude to require counteracting control; however, releasing a slight amount of back pressure on the elevator control will stop the pitch-up.

e. Standard control techniques are recommended for the execution of all stalls. Aileron control is adequate for counteracting rolling moments during both the stall and recovery. Roll due to yaw is nonexistant at the stall; consequently, all rolling moments must be counteracted by the use of the lateral controls. The airplane will pitch downward of its own accord while full up elevator is being applied during the stall; however, it is recommended that recovery be accelerated by forward movement of the elevator control when the stall occurs.

f. Stalls out of turns can be executed without the occurence of abnormal rolling moments, providing the turn is well coordinated. Stalls out of uncoordinated turns will result in increased rolling moments although sufficient lateral control is available for recovery.

g. Practice stalls can be executed with the landing gear extended with no adverse effect.

h. Recoveries from all stalls require approximately 1700 feet of altitude. Allow approximately 2500 feet for normal recovery.

2-42. SPINS.

2-43. Intentional spins are prohibited. In case a spin is entered accidentally, use normal recovery procedures to regain normal flight.

STALLING SPEED TABLE

| GROSS WEIGHT LBS | ANGLE OF BANK DEGREES | STALLING WARNING SPEED — KNOTS IAS | |
		FLAPS AND GEAR DOWN	FLAPS AND GEAR UP
162,500	0	140.5	179.0
	15	143.0	182.5
	20	145.0	184.5
	30	151.0	192.5
125,000	0	123.0	157.0
	15	125.5	160.0
	20	127.0	162.0
	30	132.5	169.0
90,000	0	104.5	133.0
	15	106.5	135.5
	20	108.0	137.5
	30	112.5	143.0

NOTE: Chart applies to altitudes below 5000 feet

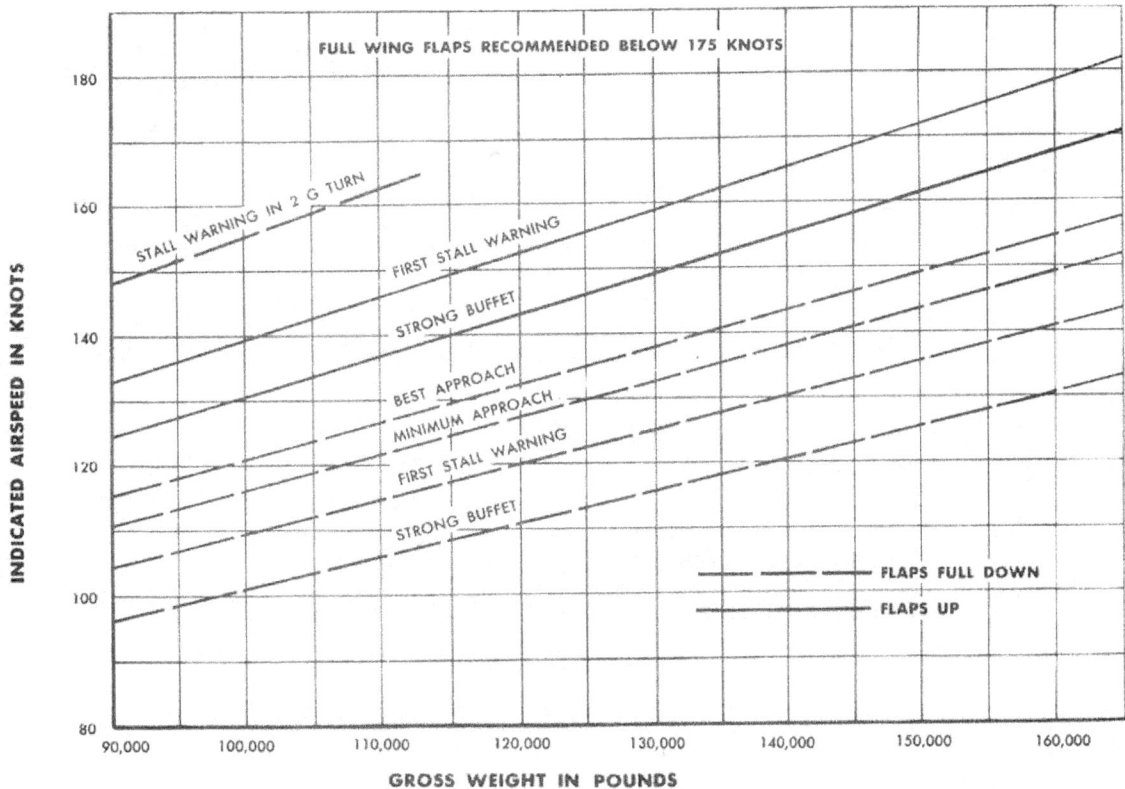

Figure 2-3. Stalling Speeds

2-44. ACROBATICS.

2-45. Acrobatics of any kind are strictly prohibited.

2-46. DIVING.

2-47. The extreme cleanness of this airplane and the fact that it is operating near the buffeting range in level flight limit it to very shallow dives which must be executed with extreme care. As with all high speed operation, abrupt accelerations must be avoided.

2-48. NIGHT FLYING.

2-49. Information will be added when available.

2-50. TURBULENT AIR AND THUNDERSTORM FLYING.

2-51. Flight through thunderstorms should be avoided if at all possible. However, since circumstances may require flight through severe turbulance, familiarization with the techniques recommended for such flight is essential.

2-52. Power settings and pitch attitude are the keys to proper flight technique in turbulent air. Obtain the power setting and pitch attitude to maintain the desired penetration speed (figure 2-4). If these are maintained throughout the storm, a constant air speed will result regardless of any false readings of the airspeed indicator.

2-53. When approaching the storm, it is imperative that the airplane be prepared prior to entry into the turbulent air. Also, it should be kept in mind that normally, the least turbulent area in a thunderstorm will be at an altitude of 6000 feet above the terrain and that altitudes between 10,000 feet and 20,000 feet are usually most turbulent. The following procedure should be used to prepare the airplane for entry into the turbulent area:

a. Disengage autopilot.
b. Pitot heat switches "ON."
c. Adjust throttles as necessary to obtain the correct penetration speed.
d. Check gyro instruments.
e. Safety belt tightened (notify crew).
f. Turn off any radio equipment rendered useless by static.
g. At night, turn cockpit lights full bright or use dark blinding glasses to minimize blinding effect of lightning.
h. Do not lower landing gear or wing flaps as they merely decrease the aerodynamic efficiency of the airplane.

2-54. When the airplane is in the storm, the following procedure should be used:

a. Maintain power settings and pitch attitude (established before entering the storm) throughout the storm. If these are held constant, the air speed will be constant regardless of the airspeed indicator reading.
b. Devote all attention to flying the airplane.
c. Expect turbulence, precipitation, and lightning; do not allow them to cause undue concern.
d. Concentrate principally on holding a level attitude by reference to the attitude gyro.

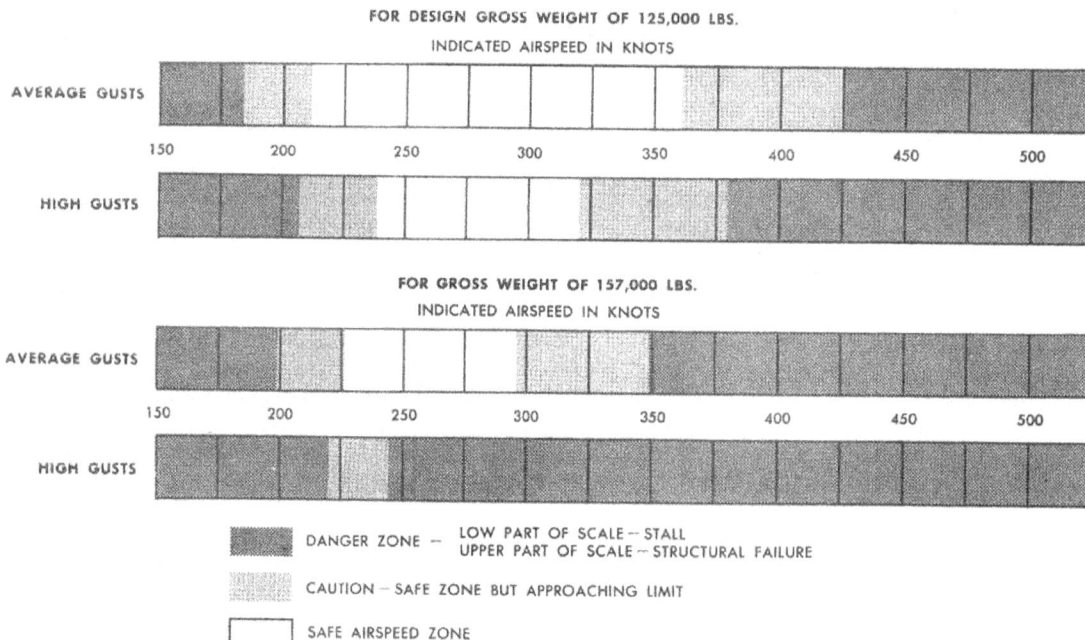

Figure 2-4. Turbulent Air Penetration Speed

e. Do not chase the airspeed indicator since doing so will result in extreme airplane attitudes. If a sudden gust should be encountered while the airplane is in a nose high attitude, a stall might easily result. A heavy rain, by partial blocking of the pitot tube pressure head, may decrease the indicated air speed reading by as much as 60 knots.

f. Use as little elevator control as possible to maintain attitude in order to minimize the stresses imposed on the airplane.

g. The altimeter is unreliable in thunderstorm flying because of differential barometric pressures within the turbulent area. A gain or loss of several thousand feet may be expected. Make allowance for this error in determining minimum safe altitude.

2-55. DESCENT.

2-56. Since jet engine fuel consumption is excessive at low altitudes, an early descent from cruising altitude will result in loss of range. Propeller airplane let-down procedures do not apply to this airplane. The normal descent procedure is as follows:

a. Maintain cruising altitude until about 45 nautical miles from landing point.

b. Extend gear.

c. Reduce power on all engines to the 35% RPM stops.

NOTE

In case Nesa deicing or K-2 system operation is being maintained, operate with sufficient power on engines 1 and 6 to supply alternator voltage.

d. Descend at the maximum rate but do not exceed Mach .82 and/or 304 knots IAS.

2-57. If a descent is made for the purpose of checking ground references, climb back to cruising altitude as soon as possible. If less than 100 miles from landing point, climb until within normal descent range. If the pilot elects to remain at low altitude, emergency engine operations must be followed to maintain optimum range from the fuel remaining.

2-58. APPROACH.

PILOT

1. Check gross weight by fuel quantity indicators; calculate CG; determine approach speed

2. Arm rests down; adjust shoulder harness and safety belt

3. Turn off K-2 radar and autopilot systems

4. Surface power control switches "ON"

5. Accomplish before landing fuel system management check

6. Wing slat warning horn switch "NORMAL"

7. Steering selector lever "TAKE-OFF, LAND"

8. Anti-skid switch "ON"

9. When required, request copilot to lower landing gear; when lowered, check four gear down and locked lights illuminated

11. When required, request copilot to lower wing flaps; when full down, check slats

12. Obtain landing clearance and set altimeter

COPILOT

1. Check weight and CG

2. Seat swivel locked; arm rests down; adjust shoulder harness and safety belt

4. Check generator voltages and load

5. Check hydraulic fluid quantity and pressures

9. On pilot's order, landing gear control lever "DN"; check four gear down and locked lights illuminated; landing gear control lever "OFF"

10. Main hydraulic system charging valve switch "PRESSURIZE"

11. On pilot's order, wing flap lever "DOWN"; when flaps are full down, wing flap lever "OFF"

12. Set altimeter

CHECK FOR CORRECT
APPROACH SPEED

REDUCE POWER
START ROUNDING
OUT OR START
GO-AROUND

TOUCH DOWN BOTH GEAR
OPEN DRAG CHUTE

WING FLAPS
FULL DOWN

APPLY BRAKES
AT 80 KNOTS

LANDING GEAR FULL DOWN ON
ENTRY INTO DOWNWIND LEG

NOTE

%RPM	GLIDE ANGLE
0	9.5/1
35	11.5/1
52	16.5/7

048017 A

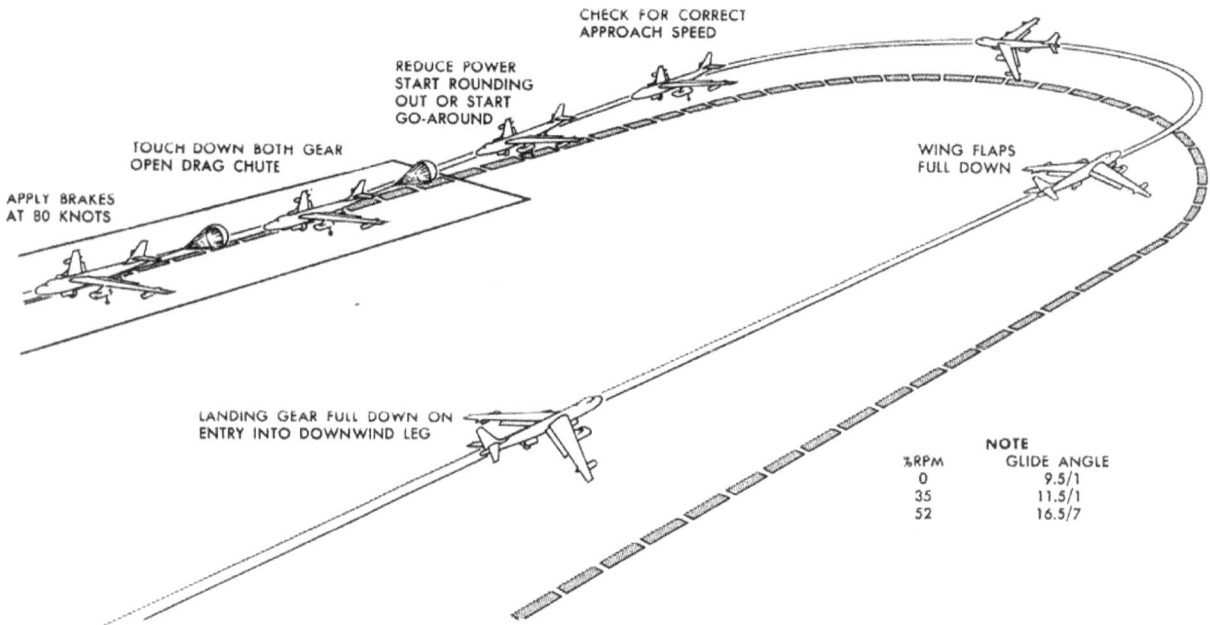

Figure 2-5. Landing Pattern

2-59. LANDING.

2-60. LANDING TECHNIQUE. The following information is presented as an aid to the pilot and represents piloting experience to date.

2-61. NORMAL LANDING. A normal landing pattern (figure 2-5) can be used. The pilot will notice a relatively flat gliding angle and slow deceleration. Approach air speeds for given gross weights must be accurately determined. Since approach air speeds are important, a sensitive air speed indicator is provided.

2-62. On final approach it is not recommended that engine RPM be decreased below 35% on all engines until the landing is assured. If there is any doubt about making a landing, RPM should be increased to 52% until the landing is assured or a go-around started.

2-63. The round out is normal with a noticeable ground effect causing the airplane to float.

2-64. Always land about 3 to 5 knots slower than the minimum approach speed, touching down with both main gear simultaneously. However, do not hold the airplane off for long as it will continue to float. Touching down with the rear gear first may be desirable; however, if the front gear is more than 3 feet off the ground when the rear gear touches, the front gear will slam down hard. A bounce will occur if the front gear touches first.

2-65. When the landing is definitely committed, retard the throttles to "CUTOFF" for engines 1, 2, 5, and 6. Taxi in on engines 3 and 4, maintaining required RPM. Turn off all possible electrical circuits while taxiing.

2-66. CROSS-WIND LANDING. A combination of crabbing into the wind and lowering the up-wind wing is recommended for landing in a cross wind. Touching an outrigger gear first is not serious because the outrigger shock struts are designed with unusually long strokes and are free castering to facilitate the most severe cross-wind landing conditions. Caution must be exercised that the up-wind wing is not lowered to the point where the outboard nacelle will drag. If possible, straighten the airplane out before touch-down.

2-67. MINIMUM RUN LANDING. The drag chute provides considerable deceleration forces over the first portion of the landing roll. With the anti-skid system operative, braking can be applied immediately on touch-down and throughout the landing roll. However, the brakes are quite ineffective until the airplane has decelerated to approximately 80 knots

at which time sufficient weight is on the wheels to allow effective braking. The drag chute should be deployed immediately upon touch-down.

NOTE

Deployment of the drag chute prior to touch-down is not recommended.

2-68. The time required for the drag chute to deploy is about 3 seconds after the deployment handle is pulled. If the chute is deployed during the flare-out, it tends to steepen the angle of approach. If deployment is attempted after the flare-out while the airplane is floating, there is a tendency for the airplane to drop-in due to the rapid deceleration caused by the chute. Therefore, the chute is to be deployed on touch-down for all landings. In all but severe cross-wind landings, the drag chute should be retained on the airplane until it reaches the line. In severe cross-wind conditions, request a ground crew to stand by to receive the chute and jettison it before taxiing in. Jettisoning is accomplished by pulling the drag chute jettison handle to the limit of travel.

2-69. EMERGENCY LANDING. For emergency landing instructions, refer to section III.

2-70. GO-AROUND. To make a go-around, open the throttles and retract the landing gear as soon as possible after it is certain that the airplane will not touch the ground. Wing flaps should be raised at the pilot's discretion. Go-around decisions should be made as early as possible since jet engine acceleration time is high and approach speeds are relatively close to touch-down speeds; hence, initial settling is more pronounced than on propeller driven airplanes.

2-71. STOPPING ENGINES.

PILOT

1. Throttles "CUTOFF"

2. Fuel selector switches "Tank-to-Engine"

3. Front gear steering selector lever - "TOW"

4. After engines stop, push fire button

COPILOT

1. All switches "OFF" (except generator switches)

048062A

───────────── 2-72. <u>BEFORE LEAVING AIRPLANE</u>. ─────────────

PILOT

1. Battery switch "OFF"

2. Remove ATO safety link

3. Ignition switches "NORMAL"

4. Surface lock lever "LOCK"

5. Wing flap lever "OFF"

6. Landing gear control lever "OFF"

7. Surface power control switches and all other switches "OFF"

8. Parking brakes off

9. Chocks in place

10. Landing gear down locks - in place

11. Safety ejection seat by inserting streamer pins

COPILOT

11. Safety ejection seat by inserting streamer pins

048063

SECTION III EMERGENCY OPERATING INSTRUCTIONS

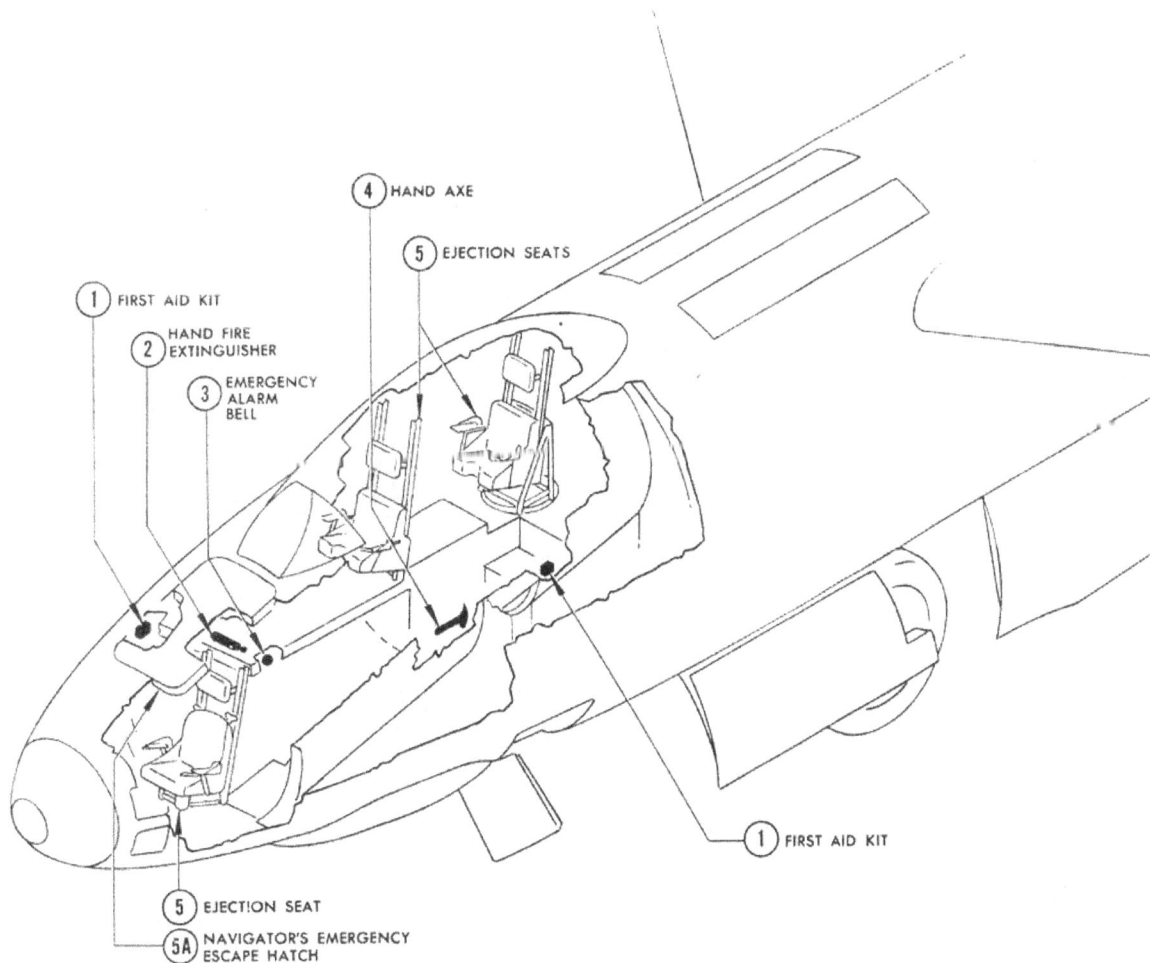

4 HAND AXE

5 EJECTION SEATS

1 FIRST AID KIT

2 HAND FIRE EXTINGUISHER

3 EMERGENCY ALARM BELL

1 FIRST AID KIT

5 EJECTION SEAT

5A NAVIGATOR'S EMERGENCY ESCAPE HATCH

Figure 3-1. Emergency Equipment

04B018 A

3-1. EMERGENCY EXITS AND ENTRANCES.

3-2. The navigator's emergency escape hatch, the canopy, and the entrance door can all be jettisoned in flight. To jettison the navigator's emergency hatch, move the navigator's emergency hatch release lever inboard. To jettison the canopy, pull either the pilot's or copilot's canopy emergency release handle. To jettison the entrance door and ladder, pull either the emergency door and ladder release handle in the walkway opposite the copilot's seat or a similar handle located adjacent to the entrance door. Entrance into the airplane in an emergency may be gained through these same three openings. To release the navigator's emergency hatch from outside the airplane, pull the exit release handle located on the left side of the fuselage just below the hatch. To release the canopy from outside the airplane, stand clear of airplane and pull the canopy exit release handle located on the left side of the fuselage just ahead of the pilot's windshield. To open the entrance door from outside the airplane, operate the normal entrance door handle. Emergency exits and entrances to be used for various conditions in flight and on the ground are shown in figure 3-2.

RECOMMENDED BAIL-OUT

WARNING

DO NOT EXIT THROUGH CANOPY
OR EMERGENCY HATCH DURING
FLIGHT WITHOUT USE OF
SEAT EJECTION

ALTERNATE BAIL-OUT

BOMB BAY BAIL-OUT

WARNING

DO NOT BAIL OUT THE ENTRANCE DOOR
UNLESS THE LANDING GEAR IS UP AND
THE LANDING GEAR AND BOMB BAY
DOORS ARE CLOSED; DO NOT BAIL OUT
THE BOMB BAY UNLESS THE REAR MAIN
LANDING GEAR IS UP AND THE DOORS
ARE CLOSED

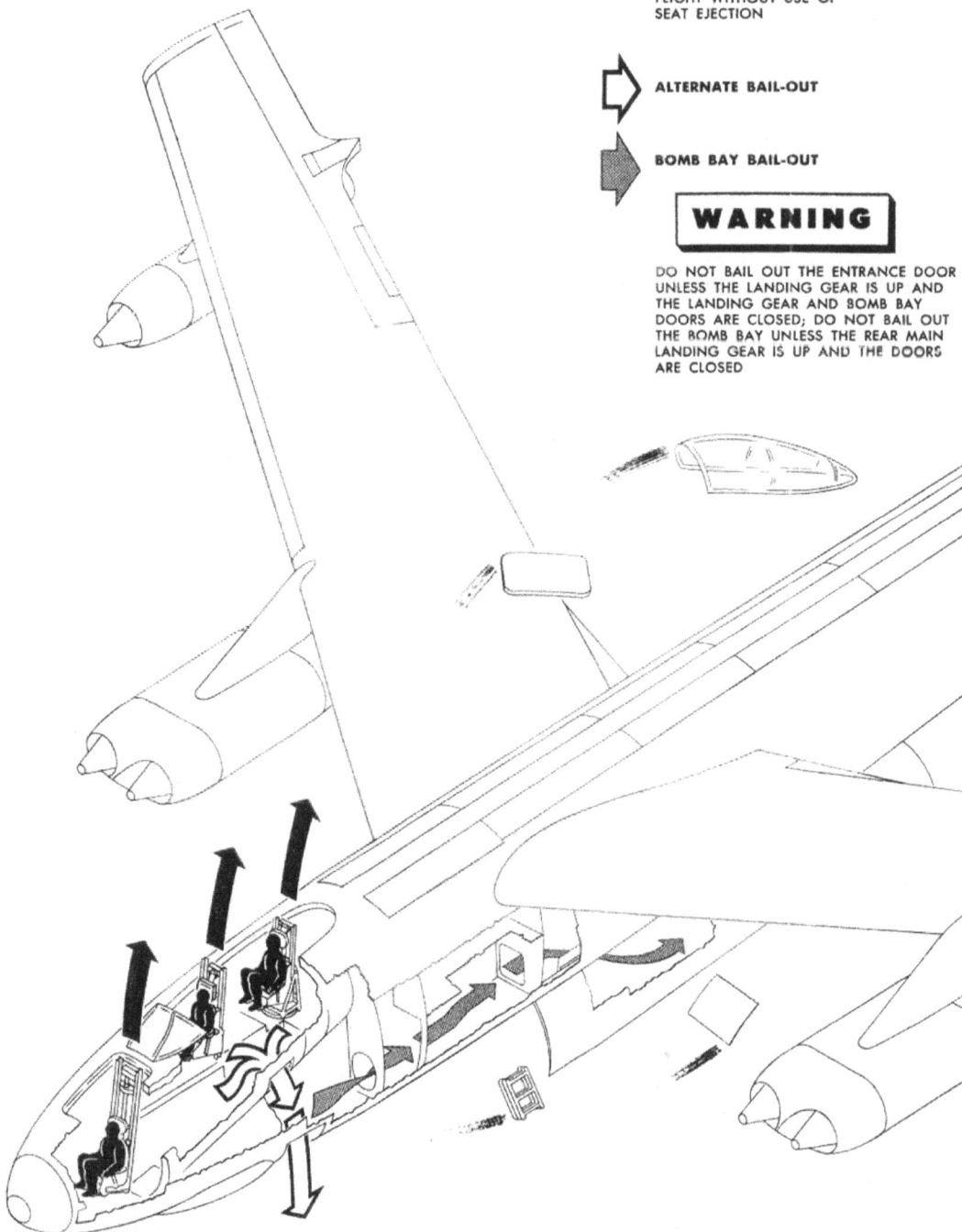

Figure 3-2 (Sheet 1 of 2 Sheets). Emergency Exits and Entrances

048019 o

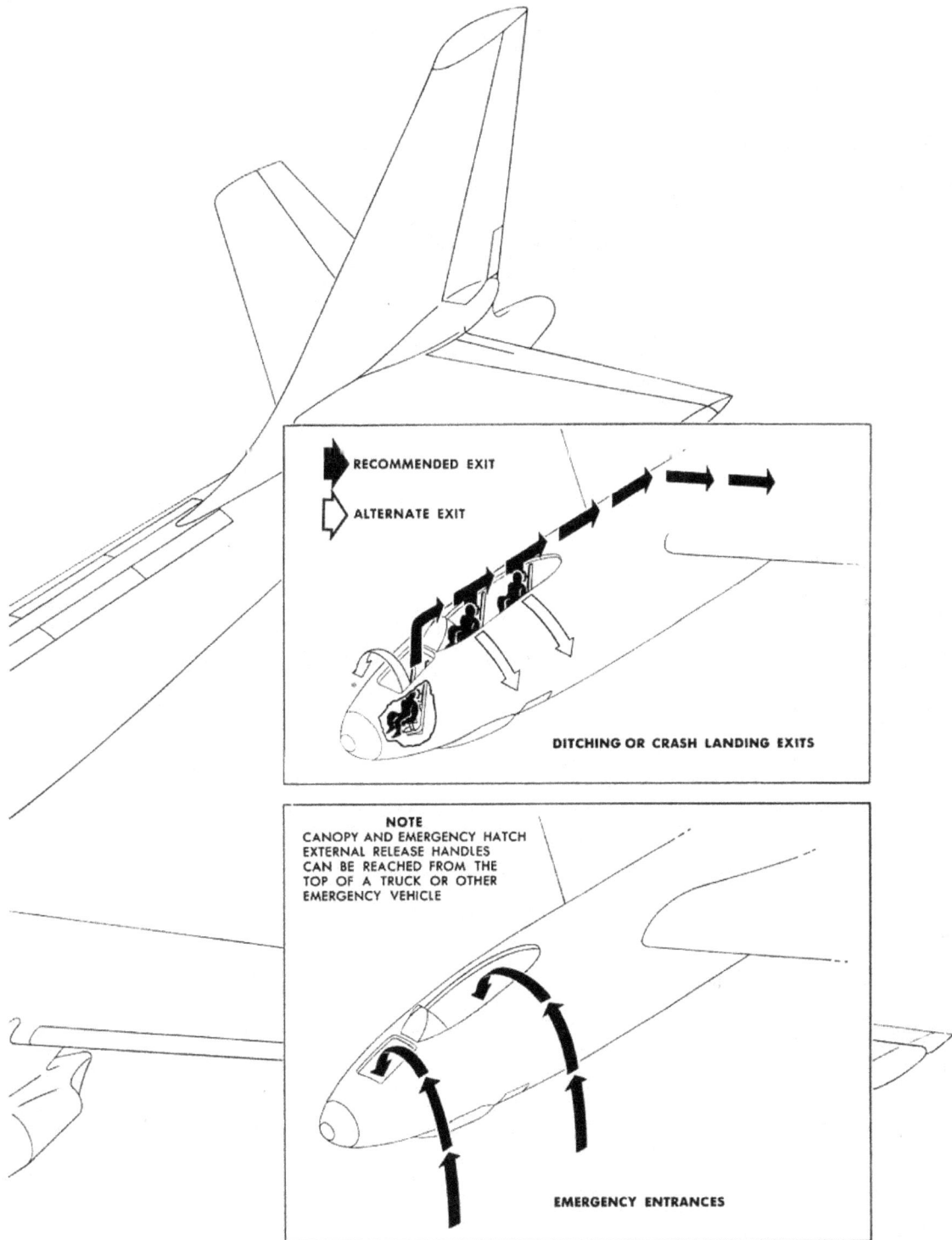

RECOMMENDED EXIT

ALTERNATE EXIT

DITCHING OR CRASH LANDING EXITS

NOTE
CANOPY AND EMERGENCY HATCH
EXTERNAL RELEASE HANDLES
CAN BE REACHED FROM THE
TOP OF A TRUCK OR OTHER
EMERGENCY VEHICLE

EMERGENCY ENTRANCES

Figure 3-2 (Sheet 2 of 2 Sheets). Emergency Exits and Entrances

048019 b

3-3. FIRE.

3-4. ENGINE FIRE DURING STARTING. An internal CO_2 system is not provided in this airplane. In case of an engine fire during starting, immediately retard the throttle for the engine on fire to "CUT-OFF," depress the fire button, position the starter switch to "CUTOFF," and the ignition switch to "OFF." Providing smoke or flame continue for an abnormal period, engage respective engine starter, leaving throttle in "CUTOFF" position. Resulting air flow through engine will remove excessive fuel and eliminate fire and/or smoke. Actuate starter switch to "CUTOFF" when fire is eliminated.

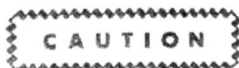

CAUTION

Use CO_2 in engine only in extreme emergencies. An accessory section louver forward of the firewall and a knockout panel aft of the firewall are the only effective points for discharge of CO_2 into the engine. Discharging CO_2 into the air intake is ineffective and may damage the engine.

3-5. ENGINE FIRE DURING FLIGHT. In case of an engine fire during flight, accomplish the following:
a. Retard throttle for the engine on fire to "CUT-OFF" and depress the fire button; this procedure will shut down the engine completely.
b. Do not attempt to restart the engine.
c. If smoke or fumes are detected in the pressurized compartment, immediately notify crew to put on oxygen masks and to position all oxygen regulator dilutor levers to "100% OXYGEN."
d. As soon as all crew members are on oxygen, pull the emergency cabin pressure release handle. If the cockpit does not immediately clear, reduce speed and open the canopy.
e. When the fire is out and the smoke dissipated, repressurize according to the instructions given in section IV, and operate the airplane according to the instructions under "Engine Failures" in paragraph 3-8.
f. Open throttle momentarily and return to "CUT-OFF" to insure engine lubrication.
g. If the fire is uncontrollable, abandon the airplane by giving spoken warning on interphone, bell warning by three short rings on the alarm bell, bail-out order on interphone, and bail-out signal by one long ring on alarm bell. See paragraph 3-35 for bail-out procedure.

3-6. FUSELAGE FIRE. A hand fire extinguisher is the only equipment provided to fight a fuselage fire. The following procedure is recommended:
a. All crew members put on oxygen masks and position their oxygen regulator dilutor levers to "100% OXYGEN."
b. If the fire is electrical in origin, turn off all unnecessary electrical equipment.
c. Apply the minimum extinguishing agent necessary at the base of the flame.

d. As soon as the fire is out, clear the cockpit of smoke and fumes by pulling the emergency cabin pressure release lever. If cockpit does not clear, reduce speed and open the canopy.
e. When the cockpit is cleared, repressurize in accordance with the instructions given in section IV.
f. If the fire is uncontrollable, abandon the airplane by giving spoken warning on interphone, bell warning by three short rings on alarm bell, bail-out order on interphone, and bail-out signal by one long ring on alarm bell. See paragraph 3-35 for bail-out procedure.

3-7. WING OR EMPENNAGE FIRE. No CO_2 system is provided to fight a wing or empennage fire. In case of a fire, proceed as follows:
a. De-energize all possible electrical circuits in the affected area.
b. When possible, attempt to sideslip airplane away from flame.
c. In the event of a wing fire in the vicinity of an outboard nacelle, retard the throttle for the respective engine to "CUTOFF," push the fire button, and position all fuel selector switches on "Tank-to-Engine." If the fire is in the inboard section of the wing, use "Tank-to-Engine" fuel management for the engines on the opposite side of the airplane, retard the throttles to "CUTOFF" for all engines on the side which is on fire, and push the fire button. Position the fuel selector switches for the inoperative engines to "Manifold-to-Engine." When the fire is extinguished, momentarily crack the throttles for the inoperative engines to restore engine lubrication. (On some airplanes, depress the nacelle close-off door button.) Do not attempt engine restart.
d. If fire occurs in the tail or empennage, turn off all electrical equipment in the area and, if operating, turn off the empennage heaters.
e. If fire is uncontrollable, abandon the airplane by giving spoken warning on interphone, bell warning by three short rings on alarm bell, bail-out order on interphone, and bail-out signal by one long ring on alarm bell. See paragraph 3-35 for bail-out procedure.

3-8. ENGINE FAILURE.

3-9. Engine failure, even of an outboard engine just at the unstick point on take-off, introduces much less yaw and mistrim than on propeller driven airplanes. Hence, with surface power control operating, engine failure presents much less of a problem in airplane control than on propeller driven airplanes. The most critical condition would be failure after the refusal IAS is reached on take-off with very high gross weights and high outside air temperature. Under these conditions, acceleration to climb speed would be slow and ability to maintain altitude during acceleration would be marginal.

3-10. ENGINE FAILURE DURING TAKE-OFF - TAKE-OFF REFUSED.
a. If maximum refusal IAS is not attained before failure, immediately retard all throttles to "IDLE," open the drag chute, and apply brakes; if stop appears

048064A

to be marginal, retard throttles to "CUTOFF" and depress the fire button.

b. If a stop cannot be made before an obstruction will be reached, and IAS is not appreciably greater than 60 knots, position the steering ratio selector to "TAXI" and ground-loop the airplane.

c. If the brakes have also failed and it becomes apparent that it will be impossible to stop or ground-loop the airplane before an obstacle is reached, as a last resort retract all landing gears by actuating the landing gear emergency retraction switch on the pilot's control stand.

d. Cut the battery switch after the landing gears retract.

e. Leave the airplane as soon as possible. To prevent possible injury caused by leaping from the airplane, use the wing as a ramp.

3-11. ENGINE FAILURE DURING TAKE-OFF -

TAKE-OFF CONTINUED. All gross weights can be sustained in flight with a single engine failure on take-off. If take-off is to be continued, proceed as follows:

a. Take-off is committed at the maximum refusal IAS. The ATO firing IAS is reached 10 seconds before the take-off point; this allows 5 seconds of ATO thrust during landing gear retraction.

b. Retract the landing gear as soon as possible.

c. If engine failure is accompanied by vibration or fire, immediately retard throttle to "CUTOFF" and depress fire button. Lesser symptoms of malfunction may permit continued operation of the engine throughout the take-off, thus allowing utilization of what thrust is being developed until cause of malfunction can be determined.

d. Start retracting flaps at approximately 25 knots above take-off velocity. Settling of the airplane is noticeable when the flaps retract beyond the 50% position if the air speed is less than approximately 170 knots. Therefore, care should be exercised in

INOPERATIVE ENGINES	PRESSURE ALTITUDE IN FEET		
	SEA LEVEL	3000	6000
Nos. 1 or 6	130 KNOTS IAS (STRONG BUFFET STALLING SPEED)	130 KNOTS IAS (STRONG BUFFET STALLING SPEED)	130 KNOTS IAS (STRONG BUFFET STALLING SPEED)
Nos. 1 and 2 or 5 and 6	139 KNOTS IAS	134 KNOTS IAS	130 KNOTS IAS (STRONG BUFFET STALLING SPEED)
Nos. 1, 2, and 3 or 4, 5, and 6	FLIGHT CANNOT BE MAINTAINED	FLIGHT CANNOT BE MAINTAINED	FLIGHT CANNOT BE MAINTAINED

BASED ON: Gross weight 162,500 lbs, flaps full down, 100% RPM on operating engines; NACA standard day

Figure 3-2A. Minimum Control Speeds with Inoperative Engines

GROSS WEIGHT IN LBS.	SERVICE CEILING IN FEET			
	ONE ENGINE INOPERATIVE	TWO ENGINES INOPERATIVE	THREE ENGINES INOPERATIVE	FOUR ENGINES INOPERATIVE
80,000	48,000	44,000	37,100	24,100
100,000	43,900	39,900	32,400	18,000
120,000	40,400	36,000	28,000	11,900
140,000	37,000	32,500	24,000	6,000
162,500	33,700	28,700	19,500	FLIGHT CANNOT BE MAINTAINED

BASED ON: Flaps and gear up, 100% RPM on operating engines; NACA standard day

Figure 3-2B. Service Ceilings with Inoperative Engines

raising the flaps beyond 50% if acceleration is extremely slow.

e. Gain a minimum of 175 knots before attempting climb.

f. Land as soon as possible.

3-12. ENGINE FAILURE DURING TAKE-OFF - FORCED LANDING. If it is impossible to maintain altitude after continued take-off with engine failure, accomplish the following:

a. If wing flaps have been raised, re-extend them to full down.

b. Battery switch "OFF."

c. Open the canopy and leave the actuating lever in the "OPEN" position. This procedure maintains hydraulic pressure in the actuating cylinder and will prevent the canopy from creeping or slamming closed during crash landing.

d. Check safety belt and lock shoulder harness inertia reel lock handle.

e. Open the drag chute when near the ground to prevent the airplane from floating.

f. Land straight ahead, changing direction only enough to miss obstacles.

g. Retard all throttles to "CUTOFF" and depress fire button just before contact.

h. Jettison navigator's hatch after airplane has stopped.

3-13. ENGINE FAILURE DURING FLIGHT.

a. Retard throttle of failed engine to "CUTOFF"; depress fire button on evidence of fire.

b. Set up airplane systems for emergency operation (see paragraphs 3-46, 3-50, and 3-55). For the service ceilings that can be attained with one or more inoperative engine, see Figure 3-2B.

c. If malfunction can be corrected, restart engine according to instructions in paragraph 3-14.

3-14. ENGINE RESTART IN FLIGHT. Engine restarts become progressively hotter with higher altitudes. Make engine accelerations and decelerations as slowly as practicable at altitude to avoid blow-out. Altitude starts should not be attempted at altitudes above 15,000 feet when using MIL-F-5616 fuel or above 25,000 feet when using MIL-F-5572 or MIL-F-5624 fuels. All restarts should be made at engine windmill RPM of 14 to 18%.

NOTE

The best altitude for restarts is 15,000 feet; therefore, if the weather and terrain permit, descend to this altitude before attempting restart.

3-15. The starter is of no use at air speeds above 150 knots IAS. Restarting procedure is as follows:

a. On loss of power, immediately close throttle and maintain airplane level for at least 5 seconds to purge engine and drain any fuel accumulation.

b. Reduce speed so that engine windmilling speed is 14 to 18% RPM.

c. Position ignition switch to "ALTITUDE START AND TEST"; do not exceed a 3-minute period in this position.

d. Rapidly open throttle to obtain 20 PSI fuel pressure and maintain fixed throttle position until ignition occurs.

NOTE

If ignition does not occur within 20 seconds after opening throttle, advance throttle to increase fuel pressure to 35 PSI, then again retard throttle to 20 PSI. Continue this procedure until engine fires or until 60 seconds total time has elapsed. If ignition still does not occur, close throttle to "CUTOFF" and do not attempt another start until after engine purging and fuel draining is completed.

e. When ignition occurs, as evidenced by an increase in exhaust temperature, maintain fuel pressure at 25 to 30 PSI until exhaust temperature begins to stabilize.

f. Advance throttle to increase fuel pressure and flow as required to maintain an exhaust temperature between 450 and 500 degrees C until normal idle RPM for that altitude is obtained. Return ignition switch to "NORMAL" and accelerate engine to desired engine speed.

3-15A. TWO-ENGINE ENDURANCE.

3-15B. Maximum endurance at altitudes below approximately 15,000 feet is attained with only two engines operating. Minimum airplane drag and minimum use of electrical equipment are the main requisites for successful two-engine endurance. For example, the landing gear and wing flaps must be retracted before shutting down engines as the electrical requirements of these items are high, and, with two engines operating, power available to sustain flight is marginal with either gear or flaps extended and inadequate if both are extended. When it is necessary to remain in the air at low altitudes for holding over destination, or other reasons, and fuel supply remaining is critical, proceed as follows:

a. Check airplane in "clean" condition (landing gear and wing flaps fully retracted).

b. Turn off all unnecessary electrical equipment. See paragraph 3-51A.

c. Retard throttles to "CUTOFF" on engine Nos. 1, 2, 5, and 6 but do not depress the fire button or the nacelle close-off door button. The nacelle close-off doors are left open because the additional drag over having the doors closed is negligible and allowing the engines to windmill will permit rapid restarts without the use of starters.

NOTE

If windshield anti-icing is required, engine Nos. 1 and 6 must be kept operating to provide alternator power for windshield anti-icing and to maintain symmetrical thrust.

d. Accomplish fuel system management to utilize all fuel and maintain airplane CG within limits by positioning the fuel selector switches for the highest level tank to "Tank-to-Engine and Manifold" and all other fuel selector switches to "Manifold-to-Engine." Because of electrical load requirements, accomplish repositioning of fuel selector switches so as to have only four boost pumps operating at any one time.

e. Establish and maintain 180 knots IAS.

⚠ CAUTION

Maintain the airplane in "clean" condition and do not attempt anything but cruise flight while operating on two engines.

f. After endurance flight period is completed and-or before making landing approach, restart remaining four engines.

g. Turn on additional electrical equipment as desired and proceed as in normal flight.

3-16. EMERGENCY LANDINGS (GROUND).

3-17. LANDING WITH FAILED ENGINE OR ENGINES.

3-18. Landings with engine failure can be accomplished by following the normal landing procedure.

3-19. Care should be exercised in the event of multi-engine failure to avoid reducing speed or altitude excessively until certain that the landing field is within range of the reduced power glide. Under these conditions, wing flaps and landing gear should not be extended until it is certain the landing area can be reached.

3-20. Under any approach conditions involving reduced power, the necessity of early anticipation of additional power requirements cannot be overemphasized.

3-21. LANDING WITH LANDING GEAR FAILURES.

3-22. If electrical extension of the landing gear with the normal system fails, emergency extension will normally be accomplished by the copilot, utilizing the mechanical emergency extension mechanism.

3-23. If emergency extension of the landing gear is impossible, the following procedure is recommended:

a. If either or both outrigger gears fail to extend, make normal landing on the main gear. Wings should be held level with ailerons as long as possible. If no cross-wind exists, the airplane will probably remain upright on the dual wheel main gear.

b. If the front or rear main landing gear cannot be extended, it is recommended that all landing gears be retracted and a wheels-up landing executed.

3-24. CRASH LANDING.

3-25. CRASH LANDING TECHNIQUE. Providing the terrain and other conditions are favorable to a successful crash landing, the following technique will be followed:

a. Burn up all fuel in auxiliary and rear main tanks and all unnecessary fuel in remaining tanks.

b. All crew members remain in seat, unbuckle parachute, but retain safety belt and shoulder harness.

c. Start a normal approach.

d. At the point in the approach where the throttles are normally retarded to "IDLE," move all throttles to "CUTOFF" and push fire button.

e. Two procedures may be followed concerning the jettisoning of the canopy. This decision is dependent upon the existing conditions and is at the discretion of the pilot. First, the canopy can be jettisoned at sufficient altitude to allow bail-out in the event the canopy strikes and damages the empennage. To minimize the probability of the canopy striking the empennage, the jettisoning operation should occur at a speed of 220 knots IAS or more. Secondly, if emergency conditions occur at low altitude and low speeds, open the canopy and leave the actuating lever in the "OPEN" position. This procedure maintains hydraulic pressure in the actuating cylinder and will prevent the canopy from creeping or slamming closed during crash landing.

f. Open drag chute at point where normal contact would occur. Without the drag chute, the airplane will float for a considerable distance.

g. Flare out just above the ground and make contact in normal landing attitude.

h. Make contact with the ground at the lowest possible air speed and rate of descent consistent with safe control of the airplane. Do not stall in.

3-26. PREPARATION FOR CRASH LANDING.

PILOT	COPILOT	NAVIGATOR
1. Give prepare-to-crash-land warning over interphone and by six short rings on alarm bell	1. Upon receiving prepare-to-crash-land warning, start emergency radio procedure	
2. Actuate bomb salvo switch and close bomb bay doors		

─────────── 3-26. PREPARATION FOR CRASH LANDING (CONTINUED). ───────────

PILOT	COPILOT	NAVIGATOR
3. Pull emergency cabin pressure release handle		
4. Check safety belt and shoulder harness fastened; unbuckle parachute	4. Check safety belt and shoulder harness fastened; unbuckle parachute	4. Check safety belt and shoulder harness fastened; unbuckle parachute
5. Providing the canopy is to be jettisoned, lower head and body as far as possible and signal copilot to release canopy, or open canopy if canopy is not jettisoned	5. Lower head and body as far as possible and watch pilot for canopy release signal	
	6. Upon signal from pilot, pull canopy emergency release handle	
7. Five seconds before contacting ground, give brace-for-crash-landing warning over the interphone and by one long sustained ring on the alarm bell		
8. Brace for crash landing and place shoulder harness inertia reel lock handle in the "LOCKED" position	8. Brace for crash landing and place shoulder harness inertia reel lock handle in the "LOCKED" position	8. Brace for crash landing and place shoulder harness inertia reel lock handle in the "LOCKED" position

CAUTION

The crew member is prevented from bending forward when the handle is in the "LOCKED" position; therefore, all switches not readily accessible should be cut before moving the handle to the "LOCKED" position.

3-27. ABANDONING THE AIRPLANE. Remain in seats until airplane comes to a stop. As soon as the airplane stops, the navigator releases the emergency escape hatch and exits through the hatch opening. The pilot and copilot exit through the canopy opening. If the emergency hatch cannot be released, the navigator proceeds aft and exits through the canopy opening. To prevent possible injury caused by leaping from the airplane, use the wing as a ramp.

3-28. LANDING WITH FRONT GEAR STEERING FAILURE. If it appears that the front gear steering system will be inoperable on landing, position the steering ratio selector lever to "TOW" and maintain directional control on landing by use of the rudder ailerons. The drag chute will help keep the airplane straight during the first part of the landing roll. Release the drag chute if it tends to swing the airplane off the landing path as speed is reduced.

3-29. LANDING WITH BRAKE FAILURE.
a. Upon touching down, immediately retard all throttles to "CUTOFF," open the drag chute, and depress the fire button.
b. If a stop cannot be made before an obstruction

will be reached, and IAS is not appreciably greater than 60 knots, position the steering ratio selector to "TAXI" and ground-loop the airplane.
c. If it becomes apparent that it will be impossible to stop or ground-loop the airplane before an obstacle is reached, as a last resort retract all landing gears by actuating the landing gear emergency retraction switch on the pilot's control stand.
d. Cut the battery switch after the landing gears retract.
e. Leave the airplane as soon as possible. To prevent possible injury caused by leaping from the airplane, use the wing as a ramp.

3-30. DITCHING.

3-31. In a properly executed ditching, the airplane's two-deck fuselage, pressurized compartment, and fuselage fuel tanks should permit the fuselage to remain afloat long enough to allow crew members to abandon the airplane. However, the high wing position, underslung engine pods, lack of wing tanks for buoyancy, and the bomb bay opening all combine to make careful handling extremely important during the ditching operation.

048060 b A

3-32. DITCHING TECHNIQUE.

a. Check landing gear fully retracted.

b. Fully extend wing flaps.

c. Remain in seats, unbuckle parachute, but retain safety belt and shoulder harness.

d. Start a normal approach.

e. At the point in the approach where the throttles are normally retarded to "IDLE," move all throttles to "CUTOFF" and push fire button.

f. Two procedures may be followed concerning the jettisoning of the canopy. This decision is dependent on the existing conditions and is at the discretion of the pilot. First, the canopy can be jettisoned at sufficient altitude to allow bail-out in the event the canopy strikes and damages the empennage. To minimize the probability of the canopy striking the empennage, the jettisoning operation should occur at a speed of 220 knots IAS or more. Secondly, if emergency conditions occur at low altitude and low speeds, open the canopy and leave the actuating lever in the "OPEN" position. This procedure maintains hydraulic pressure in the actuating cylinder and will prevent the canopy from creeping or slamming closed during ditching.

g. Choose the direction of the ditching run carefully. If a uniform wave or swell pattern exists, best results will be achieved by ditching parallel to the waves or swells. Try to touch down along the crest or just after the crest passes. The best procedure is to ditch into the wind unless high swells are running and there is very little wind.

h. Flare out just over the water and touch down in a nose high attitude. This will give the best distribution of landing shock over the fuselage. Avoid contact in nose-down attitude and be careful to keep wings level.

i. Make contact at the lowest possible air speed and rate of descent consistent with safe control of the airplane. This will reduce the landing impact. Do not stall the airplane in as this will result in severe impact.

3-33. PREPARATION FOR DITCHING.

PILOT	COPILOT	NAVIGATOR
1. Give prepare-to-ditch warning over interphone and by six short rings on alarm bell	1. Upon receiving prepare-to-ditch warning, start emergency radio procedure	
2. Actuate bomb salvo switch and close bomb bay doors		
3. Pull emergency cabin pressure release handle		
4. Check safety belt and shoulder harness fastened; unbuckle parachute; check life vest	4. Check safety belt and shoulder harness fastened; unbuckle parachute; check life vest	4. Check safety belt and shoulder harness fastened; unbuckle parachute; check life vest
5. If canopy is to be jettisoned, lower head and body as far as possible and signal copilot to release canopy, or open canopy if it is not jettisoned	5. Lower head and body as far as possible and watch pilot for canopy release signal	
	6. Upon signal from pilot, pull canopy emergency release handle	
7. Five seconds before contacting water, give brace-for-ditching warning over the interphone and by one long sustained ring on the alarm bell		
8. Brace for ditching and place shoulder harness inertia reel lock handle in the "LOCKED" position	8. Brace for ditching and place shoulder harness inertia reel lock handle in the "LOCKED" position	8. Brace for ditching and place shoulder harness inertia reel lock handle in the "LOCKED" position

CAUTION

The crew member is prevented from bending forward when the handle is in the "LOCKED" position; therefore, all switches not readily accessible should be cut before moving the handle to the "LOCKED" position.

048068 A

3-34. ABANDONING THE AIRPLANE. Remain in seats until the airplane has come to a stop. As soon as the airplane stops, the navigator releases his emergency hatch and exits through the opening while pilot and copilot exit through the canopy opening. If the emergency hatch cannot be released, the navigator proceeds aft and exits through the canopy opening. If airplane is floating, gather all emergency gear and prepare to inflate parachute life rafts but remain with airplane as long as it floats. If airplane is under water or sinking rapidly, get clear of airplane but make every effort to retain parachute for survival purposes in the life raft.

3-35. BAIL-OUT.

─────── **3-36. PREPARATION FOR BAIL-OUT.** ───────

NOTE

In all cases requiring emergency exit in flight, it is recommended that seat ejection be utilized. This method provides the most rapid means of egress and precludes the possibility of crew injury resulting from contact with any part of the airplane.

PILOT	COPILOT	NAVIGATOR
1. Give bail-out warning over interphone and by three short rings on alarm bell		
2. Pull emergency cabin pressure release handle		
3. If time permits, reduce air speed as much as possible		
4. Trim airplane for level flight and engage autopilot		
5. Place seat in lowest position; check that keeper pins have engaged	5. Face seat forward and place in lowest position; check that keeper pins have engaged	5. Face seat forward and place in lowest position; check that keeper pins have engaged

NOTE

Seat must be in lowest position to insure sufficient acceleration for safe ejection.

PILOT	COPILOT	NAVIGATOR
6. Stow control column	6. Stow control column	
7. Check safety belt and shoulder harness fastened	7. Check safety belt and shoulder harness fastened	7. Check safety belt and shoulder harness fastened
8. Lower head and body as far as possible and signal copilot to release canopy	8. Lower head and body as far as possible and watch pilot for canopy release signal	
	9. Upon signal from pilot, pull canopy emergency release handle	
10. Raise arm rests to uppermost position	10. Raise arm rests to uppermost position	10. Raise arm rests to uppermost position

048069a

—————— 3-36. PREPARATION FOR BAIL-OUT (CONTINUED). ——————

PILOT	COPILOT	NAVIGATOR

PILOT

11. Give abandon airplane signal over interphone and by one long ring on alarm bell

12. Turn firing lever knob

C A U T I O N

Turning firing lever knob permanently locks the shoulder harness inertia reel. The pilot is prevented from bending forward when the reel is locked therefore, all switches not readily accessible should be cut before turning the firing lever knob

13. Brace head, feet, and arms against rests; press knees together

14. Raise firing lever

15. After clearing airplane, release safety belt and shoulder harness; break free of seat as soon as possible

COPILOT

12. Turn firing lever knob

C A U T I O N

Turning firing lever knob permanently locks the shoulder harness inertia reel. The copilot is prevented from bending forward when the reel is locked therefore, all switches not readily accessible should be cut before turning the firing lever knob

13. Brace head, feet, and arms against rests; press knees together

14. After pilot has cleared airplane, raise firing lever

15. After clearing airplane, release safety belt and shoulder harness; break free of seat as soon as possible

NAVIGATOR

NOTE

When the navigator's hatch is jettisoned in flight, the possibility exists that it will hit the canopy; therefore, the navigator must not release the hatch and use his seat ejection until after the pilot and copilot have abandoned the airplane

14. After pilot and copilot have cleared airplane, move emergency hatch release lever

16. Turn firing lever knob

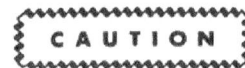

C A U T I O N

Turning firing lever knob permanently locks the shoulder harness inertia reel; the navigator is prevented from bending forward when the reel is locked; therefore, all switches not readily accessible should be cut before turning the firing lever knob

17. Brace head, feet, and arms against rests; press knees together

18. Raise firing lever

19. After clearing airplane, release safety belt and shoulder harness; break free of seat as soon as possible

WARNING

Do not exit through canopy or emergency hatch openings in flight without use of seat ejection.

048069 b A

3-37. ALTERNATE BAIL-OUT. If, for any reason, it is impossible to utilize seat ejection, escape may be made through the entrance door opening. In order to leave the airplane in this manner slow down the airplane as much as possible, pull the emergency cabin pressure release handle, pull one of the exit door and ladder release handles, trim the airplane for straight and level flight, engage the autopilot, and bail out. The navigator leaves first, followed by the copilot and pilot, in that order.

WARNING

Do not bail out the entrance door unless main landing gear, main landing gear doors, and bomb bay doors are fully retracted.

3-38. BAIL-OUT THROUGH BOMB BAY. Due to the distance of the bomb bay from the crew members stations and the small passageway to be negotiated in reaching it, exit out the bomb bay is possible only when considerable time is available and the airplane is controllable. In order to leave the airplane in this manner, reduce air speed as much as possible, actuate bomb salvo switch, pull the emergency cabin pressure release handle, trim the airplane for straight and level flight, engage the autopilot, proceed aft of the platform in the bomb bay, and bail out. The navigator leaves first, followed by the copilot and pilot, in that order.

WARNING

Do not bail out of the bomb bay unless the rear main landing gear and doors are fully retracted.

3-39. EMERGENCY GROUND STARTING ON BATTERY.

3-40. If external power is not available for starting, proceed as follows:
a. Turn off all equipment requiring DC power.
b. Position generator switch for first engine to be started to "ON."
c. Turn battery switch "ON."
d. Start first engine, using normal starting procedure.
e. Position generator switch for first engine started to "OFF" and generator switch for second engine to be started to "ON"; start second engine in the same manner as the first.
f. Repeat procedure for the third engine to be started.
g. Before starting the fourth engine, position the generator switches for the three operating engines and the engine to be started to "ON," the battery switch to "OFF," and start remaining engines on generator DC power from the three operating engines.

CAUTION

Generator loads should be evenly distributed before using generator power for starting to avoid blowing current limiters.

3-41. EMERGENCY TAXIING.

3-42. In case of front gear steering failure, directional control of the airplane cannot be maintained during taxiing. Discontinue taxiing and request to be towed.

3-43. OPERATION WITH SURFACE POWER CONTROL FAILURE.

3-44. The surface power control systems on this airplane are designed so that at approximately 260 knots IAS there should be little or no change in trim resulting from a surface power control system failure. At higher and lower air speeds, large out-of-trim control forces can occur when a surface power control system fails. These forces increase to a maximum at limiting air speeds.

3-45. If one or more of the surface power control systems fail, proceed as follows:
a. If control forces are excessive, call for copilot's aid in holding controls and in trimming the airplane.
b. Position the surface power control switch for the malfunctioning system to "OFF"; if one aileron system has failed, position both aileron surface power control switches to "OFF."

3-46. FUEL SYSTEM EMERGENCY OPERATION.

3-47. OPERATION WITH BOOST PUMP FAILURE. One boost pump per engine is sufficient for all operations except take-off and high altitude flight at high power settings. Fuel pressure in the manifold is obtained, for a take-off safety factor, by positioning the No. 2 engine fuel selector switch to "Tank-to-Engine and Manifold." If one or both boost pumps for an engine fail on take-off, position the fuel selector switches (figure 3-3) as follows:
a. Fuel selector switch for malfunctioning engine on "Manifold-to-Engine."
b. As soon as a safe altitude is reached, fuel selector switch for engine opposite the malfunctioning engine on "Tank-to-Engine and Manifold."
c. Reposition No. 2 engine fuel selector switch to "Tank-to-Engine." This will maintain equal fuel consumption from main tanks during flight.
d. If the boost pumps for No. 2 engine fail, position the fuel selector switch for No. 5 engine to "Tank-to-Engine and Manifold," and the fuel selector switch for No. 2 engine to "Manifold-to-Engine."

3-48. OPERATION WITH FUEL LINE FAILURE. If loss of boost pressure occurs under conditions that indicate a broken fuel line, accomplish the following:
a. Fuel selector switch for the malfunctioning engine on "Manifold-to-Engine."
b. If boost pressure loss then occurs for the boost pumps supplying the manifold, the break is outboard of the manifold valve. In this case, reposition the fuel selector switch for the malfunctioning engine to "Tank-to-Engine," retard the throttle to "CUTOFF," and depress the fire button.

048071A

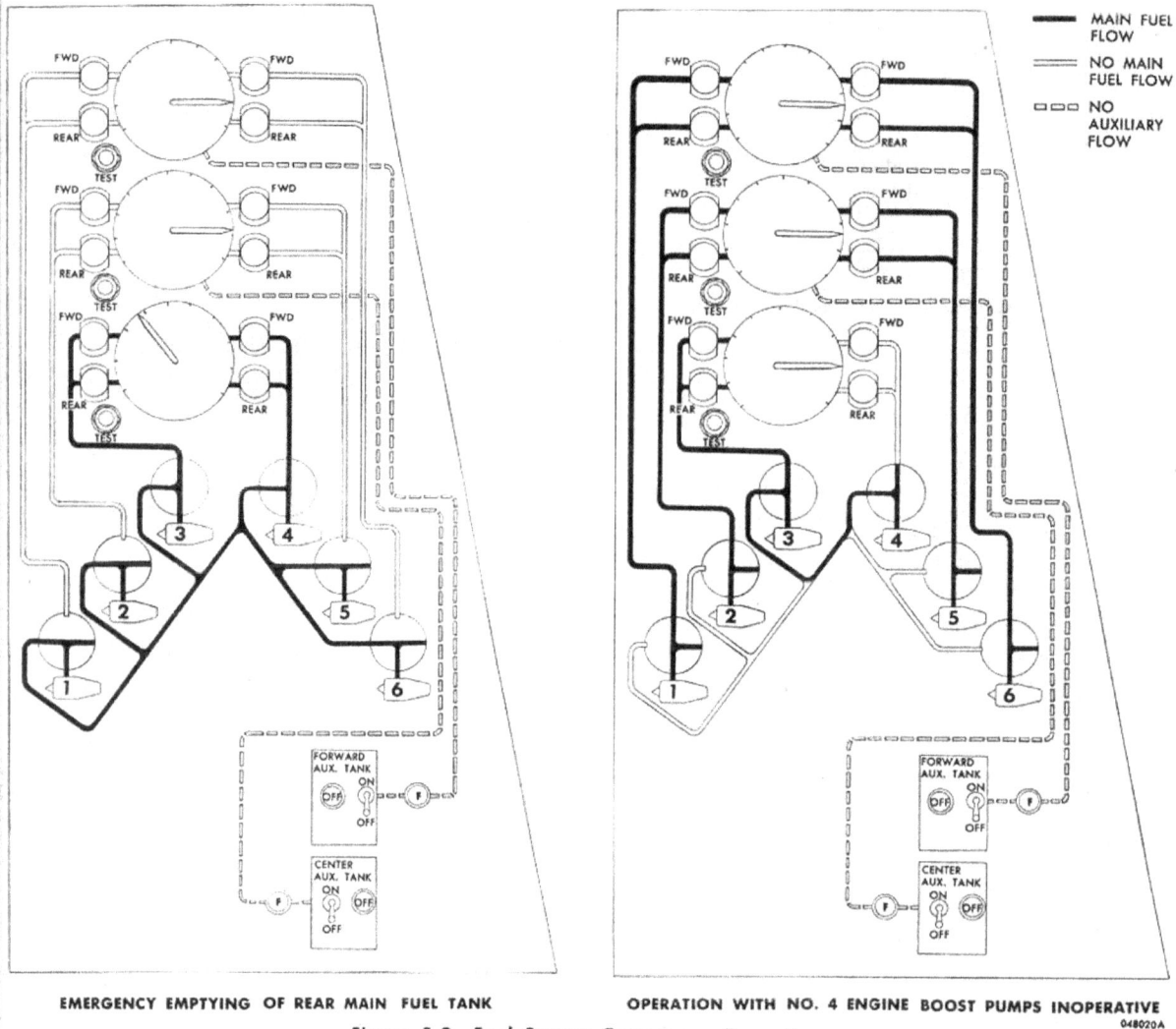

MAIN FUEL FLOW

NO MAIN FUEL FLOW

NO AUXILIARY FLOW

EMERGENCY EMPTYING OF REAR MAIN FUEL TANK

OPERATION WITH NO. 4 ENGINE BOOST PUMPS INOPERATIVE

Figure 3-3. Fuel System Emergency Operation

3-49. EMERGENCY TANK EMPTYING. In case it becomes necessary to empty one main rank rapidly, position the fuel selector switches for the engines receiving fuel from that tank to "Tank-to-Engine and Manifold." Then position all other fuel selector switches to "Manifold-to-Engine." When the tank is empty, position the fuel selector switches for the empty tank to "Manifold-to-Engine" and all other fuel selector switches to "Tank-to-Engine and Manifold."

3-50. ELECTRICAL SYSTEM EMERGENCY OPERATION.

3-51. GENERATOR FAILURE. If the generator over-voltage lights indicate that a generator has tripped off the line, the generator may be reset, if it is absolutely needed, by positioning the respective generator switch to "RESET." If two or more generators be-

come inoperative, a careful check of the load on the remaining generator should be made. Many electrical loads are not absolutely essential and may be momentarily or permanently removed from the line during emergency conditions. The table in figure 3-4 shows the approximate power requirements for the main electrical loads. Each generator is rated at 400 amps with an overload rating of 600 amps for a 5-minute period. Total the loads for any operation and check against the power available to determine if any loads must be removed from the line. The most critical partial generator operation likely to be encountered is for two-engine endurance; the detailed procedure for this is given below.

NOTE

Any tabulation of electrical loads must be an approximation or an average because loads vary with existing conditions and with the age of the equipment.

3-51A. OPERATION WITH TWO GENERATORS. Operation with only two generators, as encountered during two-engine endurance flight, requires careful consideration of the limited electrical power available. However, if all non-essential electrical equipment is turned off, sufficient electrical power is available from the remaining two generators to operate essential equipment. In addition, should one of these generators fail, the overload capacity (600 amps for 5 minutes) of the remaining generator is sufficient to operate the essential equipment until another engine can be restarted.

3-51B. The following tabulation is taken from the chart in figure 3-4 and lists the essential electrical loads and the standby loads for two-engine endurance and their average amperage requirements. This equipment must be operating, or electrical power must be available for its operation at all times:

ITEM	AMPERES
Surface power control system	183
Hydraulic accumulator heat	14
Instruments and instrument panel vibrators	5
Autopilot	9
Pitot heat	9
Flying suits	12 (average)
Lighting	26
Main inverter	68
Battery charging	15 (approx.)
Fuel boost pumps (4)	185
Radio equipment	15 (approx.)
Generator field and control	20
Canopy defrost	11
Total essential and standby load	572
Two-engine generator capacity	800
Single engine generator overload capacity (50 per cent overload for 5 minutes)	600

3-51C. A study of the complete listing of major electrical equipment items (figure 3-4) will show that the operation of starters, unnecessary fuel boost pumps, A-2 fire control, K-2 radar, wing flaps, landing gear, and hydraulic equipment must be avoided during two-engine flight. However, certain other equipment, such as the nose defroster, may be operated if the need is urgent and the total amperage load is kept to a minimum. It is recommended that the total amperage of equipment operated should not be allowed to exceed the 600 amp overload capacity of a single generator.

3-52. INVERTER FAILURE. If the spare inverter does not start automatically after a main or secondary inverter failure, place the inverter switch for the affected bus to the "SPARE INVERTER" position.

3-53. In the event that both main and secondary inverters fail and certain secondary bus loads are momentarily required, place the main bus inverter switch in the "OFF" position.

3-54. MAIN ALTERNATOR FAILURE. If the main alternator should fail or the No. 1 engine should be shut down or fail, turn the alternator selector switch to the "SPARE" position to operate the spare alternator provided that the No. 6 engine is operating.

3-55. HYDRAULIC SYSTEM EMERGENCY OPERATION.

3-56. Whenever main system pressure falls below emergency system pressure, shuttle valves are automatically actuated causing the emergency system to supply the actuating units. If emergency system pressures are not between 2700 and 3000 PSI when the emergency hydraulic pump switch is in "AUTO" and the circuit breaker is depressed, hold the switch "ON." In the "ON" position a pressure switch is by-passed and pressure should build up to 3450 PSI.

3-57. LANDING GEAR EMERGENCY OPERATION.

3-58. The landing gear can be retracted by a master hot wire switch at the pilot's station or by individual hot wire switches at the copilot's station. Except in an extreme emergency where it is necessary to immediately retract the gear, use the individual retraction switches at the copilot's station.

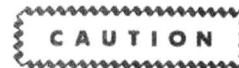

CAUTION

Hot wire circuits by-pass all limit switches. Release the switches from the "GEAR UP" position immediately when the amber gear up and locked light comes on.

3-59. In case the landing gear fails to extend, accomplish the following:
a. Move one landing gear emergency extension selector lever, aft of the copilot's seat to "ENGAGE."
b. Operate the landing gear emergency extension ratchet lever, adjacent to the selector levers, a few pulls to unlock the gear.
c. Allow the gear to free fall. To insure that the gear has locked, operate the ratchet lever until a resistance is felt.
d. Return the first selector lever to "DISENGAGE" and repeat procedure for the remaining three gears.
e. Check that the landing gear warning lights indicate the gear is down locked.
f. In case it is impossible to lower all of the landing gear, follow the required emergency landing procedure.

NOTE

If the landing gear fails to fall free when using the emergency system, longitudinal rocking of the airplane may assist in breaking it loose.

048072

3-60. WING FLAP EMERGENCY OPERATION.

3-61. The wing flaps, when extended, provide a minimum of drag and their only limiting effect on the airplane is the flap limit speed. The flaps are retracted or extended in an emergency by actuating the emergency flap switches. Slow retraction is accomplished by placing either switch, primary or secondary motor, to "UP." Rapid retraction is accomplished by placing both switches simultaneously to "UP." Rapid extension is always provided regardless of which switch is placed in "DOWN." The wing flap emergency switches by-pass all limit switches and must be released to "OFF" when the flaps reach their full travel.

WARNING

Retract the wing flaps with only one emergency switch at a time. The use of both emergency switches simultaneously results in considerable loss of lift and the airplane will settle rapidly.

3-62. BRAKE SYSTEM EMERGENCY OPERATION.

3-63. Hydraulic pressure for emergency operation of the brakes is automatically supplied by the emergency hydraulic system. Emergency brakes are applied by depressing the rudder pedals farther than is normally necessary.

EQUIPMENT	NO. UNITS	AMPS PER UNIT	TAKE-OFF CLIMB	CRUISE	CRUISE COMBAT	DESCENT LANDING
ARMAMENT AND BOMBING						
A-2 fire control (standby)	1			00	39	
Tail turret	1			143	152	
CONTROL SURFACES						
Flaps (extend)	2	75				150
Flaps (retract)	1	130	130			
Surface power control	3	61	183	183	183	183
Autopilot	1	9		9	9	
INSTRUMENTS						
Instruments and vibrators	ALL		5	5	5	5
LANDING GEAR						
Fwd main (retract)	2	155	310			
Fwd main (extend)	1	negligible				
Aft main (retract)	2	130	260			
Aft main (extend)	1	negligible				
Outriggers (retract)	2	160	320			
Outriggers (extend)	2	negligible				
HEAT, VENT, AND ANTI-ICE						
Canopy defrost	1	11	11	11	11	11
Nose defrost	1	11	11	11	11	11
Heated suit	3	9.8				
Pitot heat	2	4.5		9	9	
ENGINE CONTROLS					175	
Starter (windmilling engine)					approx	
LIGHTS						
Interior lighting (night)			24	26	8	24
Interior lighting (day)			8	8	8	8
Landing lights	2	21.5				43

GENERATOR CAPACITY

NORMAL: SIX GENERATORS AT 400 AMPS EACH, 2400 AMPS.
OVERLOAD (5 MIN.): SIX GENERATORS AT 600 AMPS EACH, 3600 AMPS.

NOTE: Red figures indicate essential loads

Figure 3-4 (Sheet 1 of 2 Sheets). Major D. C. Electrical Loads

948093u A

EQUIPMENT	NO. UNITS	AMPS PER UNIT	TAKE-OFF CLIMB	CRUISE	CRUISE COMBAT	DESCENT LANDING
HYDRAULICS						
Accumulator heat	4	14		14	14	
Emergency pump	1	150				
ELECTRICAL POWER						
Inverter, main	1	100	50	68	68	50
Inverter, secondary	1	100	50	100	100	50
Inverter, spare	1	100				
Inverter, radar				32	32	
Battery charging		15	15	15	15	15
Generator field and control	6	10	60	60	60	60
FUEL						
Fuel boost	12		600	558	568	550
Fuel transfer	2		49	49		
RADIO						
Miscellaneous		15	15	15	15	22
RADAR						
K-2 system	1	37.2		37.2	37.2	

GENERATOR CAPACITY

NORMAL: SIX GENERATORS AT 400 AMPS EACH, 2400 AMPS.
OVERLOAD (5 MIN.): SIX GENERATORS AT 600 AMPS EACH, 3600 AMPS.

NOTE: Red figures indicate essential loads

Figure 3-4 (Sheet 2 of 2 Sheets). Major D. C. Electrical Loads

048093b

SECTION IV OPERATIONAL EQUIPMENT

4-1. CABIN HEATING, VENTILATING, AND PRESSURIZING SYSTEM.

4-2. GENERAL.

4-3. Hot compressed air for cabin heating, ventilating, and pressurizing (figure 4-1) is supplied from the last stage of the Nos. 1, 2, and 3 jet engine compressors. The air is supplied to the cabin through a flow-limiting venturi tube and is ducted to outlets at the individual crew stations. The cabin is heated by a mixture of hot engine compressor air and engine compressor air cooled by an expansion type refrigeration system. The ratio of hot and cold air is controlled by an electrically operated cabin air valve to maintain a desired cabin air temperature. The cabin can also be ventilated without pressurization by ram air during flight or ground operation. A ram air blower operates automatically to supply air when ram air cabin ventilation is desired with the airplane on the ground. Cabin pressurization is maintained by a cabin pressure regulator which controls the escape of cabin air to the atmosphere. The following cabin pressure conditions are provided by the pressure regulator:

a. Unpressurized range, sea level to 5000 feet, atmosphere pressure.

b. Isobaric range, 5000 to 24,100 feet, 5000-foot altitude pressure.

c. High differential pressure range, above 24,100 feet, 6.55 PSI constant differential pressure.

d. Combat range, above 10,500 feet, 2.35 PSI constant differential pressure.

4-4. Other units of the system include a hot air shutoff valve, a ram air shutoff valve, a pressure regulating valve to reduce the hot air pressure from the engines to 1/2 PSI above cabin pressure, a pressure ratio control valve to prevent overspeeding of the refrigeration unit turbine wheel, a muffler to dampen turbine and duct noises, a spill valve to spill air into the cabin when one or more crew station air outlets are closed, and two cabin pressure relief valves to relieve cabin pressure above 6.55 PSI in the event the cabin pressure regulator should fail. These pressure relief valves also serve as emergency cabin pressure release valves to quickly depressurize the cabin, and as vacuum relief valves whenever cabin pressure is less than atmospheric pressure. Circuit breakers for the cabin air conditioning system are located on the copilot's circuit breaker panel (3, figure 1-24) and the AC circuit breaker panel (2, figure 1-24).

4-5. CONTROLS.

4-6. MASTER AIR CONDITIONING SWITCH. The master air conditioning switch (4, figure 1-11) is on the pilot's switch panel. When the switch is in the "ON" position, DC and AC power is supplied to energize the circuits and equipment so that the heat-

ing, ventilating, and pressurizing systems will be operable. When the switch is in the "OFF" position, circuits are de-energized to make the air conditioning systems inoperative and DC power is supplied to close the hot air shutoff valve, open the ram air shutoff valve, and run the cabin air valve to the off position (hot air outlet closed and cold air outlet open).

4-7. HEAT SELECTOR SWITCH. The heat selector switch (6, figure 1-8) is on the pilot's instrument panel and is marked "OFF--AUTO--COLD--HOT." When in "COLD" and "HOT" the switch is spring-loaded to "OFF." The switch is used to select automatic or manual cabin temperature regulation. When the switch is in the "OFF" position, no temperature regulation is provided and cabin temperature will be determined by the outside air temperature and the cabin air valve which will be at its last operating position. In the "AUTO" position, the switch connects DC power to the cabin temperature regulator which will automatically control the cabin air valve operation to maintain the selected cabin air temperature. In the "COLD" position, the switch supplies power directly to run the cabin air valve to reduce cabin temperature by increasing the flow of cold air and decreasing the flow of hot air. In the "HOT" position, the switch supplies power directly to run the cabin air valve to increase cabin temperature by increasing the flow of hot air and decreasing the flow of cold air.

4-8. CABIN TEMPERATURE SELECTOR RHEOSTAT. The cabin temperature selector rheostat (7, figure 1-8) is on the pilot's instrument panel and is knob controlled. Knob rotation is marked "DEC" for counterclockwise direction and "INC" for clockwise direction. When the knob is rotated in the "INC" or "DEC" direction, with the heat selector switch in the "AUTO" position, the automatically controlled temperature will be correspondingly increased or decreased as a result of the repositioning of the cabin air valve by the cabin temperature regulator.

4-9. HEAT SELECTOR KNOBS. Heat selector knobs (figure 4-1) are located at the navigator's, pilot's, and copilot's stations to provide each crew member with a means of controlling the air flow at his station. The knobs are marked "LOWER AIR--OFF--UPPER AIR" and, through mechanical linkage, operate air flow valves to direct the air to the floor outlets, shut off the air flow, or direct the air to the face outlets when the knobs are in the corresponding positions. Increasing the amount that the knob is turned away from the "OFF" position will increase the air flow at the respective outlets. When any selector knob is turned "OFF" or the air flow is limited by the selector position, the spill valve (figure 4-1) will expel the excess air into the cabin to maintain the proper air flow for pressurization.

048067

4-10. CABIN AIR SELECTOR SWITCH. The cabin air selector switch (5, figure 1-11) is on the pilot's switch panel and is marked "COMPR--RAM." The switch is used to select engine compressor air for cabin heating and pressurizing or ram air for cabin ventilating. When the switch is in the "COMPR" position, DC power is supplied to the heat selector switch for cabin heating control. When the cabin air selector switch is in the "RAM" position, DC power is disconnected from the cabin heating control system, power is supplied to open the ram air shutoff valve and close the hot air shutoff valve. Also, if the airplane is on the ground, power will be supplied to operate a ram air blower (figure 4-1).

4-11. CABIN PRESSURE REGULATION SELECTOR SWITCH. A cabin pressure regulation selector switch (6, figure 1-11) is on the pilot's switch panel and is marked "NORMAL--COMBAT." When the switch is in the "NORMAL" position, the cabin pressure regulator will function to provide atmospheric, isobaric, and high (6.55 PSI) differential pressure range regulation of cabin pressure. When the switch is in the "COMBAT" position, the cabin pressure regulator will function to provide atmospheric and isobaric range regulation to approximately 10,500 feet, and low (2.35 PSI) differential pressure regulation above 10,500 feet.

4-12. EMERGENCY CABIN PRESSURE RELEASE HANDLE. An emergency cabin pressure release handle (13, figure 1-13) is located just aft of the pilot's control stand and provides a means of quick cabin pressure release. When the handle is pulled up, the cabin pressure relief valve (figure 4-1) is opened by cable linkage and dumps cabin air into the forward wheel well and a pressure dump valve switch is actuated. When the pressure dump valve switch is actuated, DC power is connected to open the ram air shutoff valve, close the hot air shutoff valve, and operate the ram air blower if the airplane is on the ground. DC power is also disconnected from the cabin heating control system. Cabin pressurizing and heating is restored by pushing the release handle down.

4-13. HEAT RESET BUTTON. A heat reset button (14, figure 1-13) is just forward and inboard of the emergency cabin pressure release handle at the pilot's station. The heat reset button is used to restore heating when the cabin is depressurized after the emergency cabin pressure release handle is pulled up. The button, when pushed down, will reset the pressure dump valve switch to supply power to close the ram air shutoff valve, open the hot air shutoff valve, and re-energize the heat control system. Also, the ram air blower, if operating, will be de-energized.

4-14. INDICATORS.

4-15. CABIN AIR THERMOMETER. A cabin air thermometer (25, figure 1-8) is on the right side of the pilot's instrument panel. The instrument is calibrated to indicate cabin temperature in degrees centigrade.

4-16. CABIN ALTIMETER. A cabin altimeter (1, figure 1-8) is on the left side of the pilot's instrument panel. The instrument is vented to cabin air to indicate the cabin pressure altitude.

4-17. NORMAL OPERATION.

4-18. CABIN HEATING. Any or all of engines 1, 2, and 3, when operating, will supply hot compressed air for cabin heating.
  a. With DC power on, check for proper secondary regulated AC bus voltage.
  b. Check to see that the emergency cabin pressure release handle is pushed down or if heating without pressurizing is desired, check to see that the heat reset button is pressed down and the emergency cabin pressure release handle is pulled up.
  c. Check to see that the cabin air selector switch is in the "COMPR" position.
  d. Turn the master air conditioning switch to the "ON" position.
  e. Turn the heat selector switch to the "AUTO" position.
  f. Allow sufficient time for the cabin temperature to stabilize, then turn the cabin temperature selector rheostat toward "INC" or "DEC" as required to obtain the desired cabin temperature.

NOTE

Cabin heating cannot be turned off without pressurization being off also. Maximum cooling is obtained when the cabin temperature selector rheostat is in the extreme counterclockwise or "DEC" position.

4-19. RAM AIR CABIN VENTILATING (BELOW 5,000 FEET). With the master air conditioning switch in the "ON" position, place the cabin air selector switch in the "RAM" position or pull the emergency cabin pressure release handle. The latter procedure is recommended when it is planned to continue on ram air ventilation after reaching 5,000 feet.

4-20. RAM AIR CABIN VENTILATING (5,000 FEET AND ABOVE). With the master air conditioning switch in the "ON" position, pull the emergency cabin pressure release handle.

NOTE

Since the cabin pressure regulator will close at 5,000 feet, this procedure must be used at that altitude and above to insure an adequate flow of ram air.

4-21. CABIN PRESSURIZING. Any or all of engines 1, 2, and 3 will supply the quantity of air required to pressurize the cabin.
  a. Check to see that the emergency cabin pressure release handle is pushed down.

048070 A

LEGEND

HOT COMPRESSED AIR

HOT AIR TO BE COOLED

LOW PRESSURE HOT AIR

COLD AIR

VENTILATING RAM AIR

CONDITIONED AIR

CABIN PRESSURE REGULATOR

NAVIGATOR'S STATION

PILOT'S STATION

HEAT SELECTOR KNOB

COPILOT'S STATION

AIR FLOW CONTROL VALVE

CABIN AIR CONDITIONING
MASTER AIR PRESS
ON COMPR NORMAL
OFF RAM COMBAT
SUPPLY

PILOT'S SWITCH PANEL

OVER-BOARD

REFRIGERATION UNIT

RAM AIR

RAM AIR BLOWER

RAM AIR SHUTOFF VALVE

MUFFLER

GUNNER'S STATION

SPILL VALVE

EMERGENCY CABIN PRESSURE RELEASE HANDLE

HEAT RESET

P.D.V.S.

PRESSURE DUMP VALVE SWITCH

MECHANICAL LINKAGE

PRESSURE RATIO VALVE

CABIN TEMPERATURE SELECTOR

DEC INC
AUTO
HOT COLD
HEAT SELECTOR

CABIN TEMPERATURE REGULATOR

PRESSURE REGULATOR

CABIN AIR VALVE

HOT AIR SHUTOFF VALVE

CABIN PRESSURE RELIEF VALVES

VENTURI TUBE

ENGINE NO. 1

ENGINE NO. 2

ENGINE NO. 3

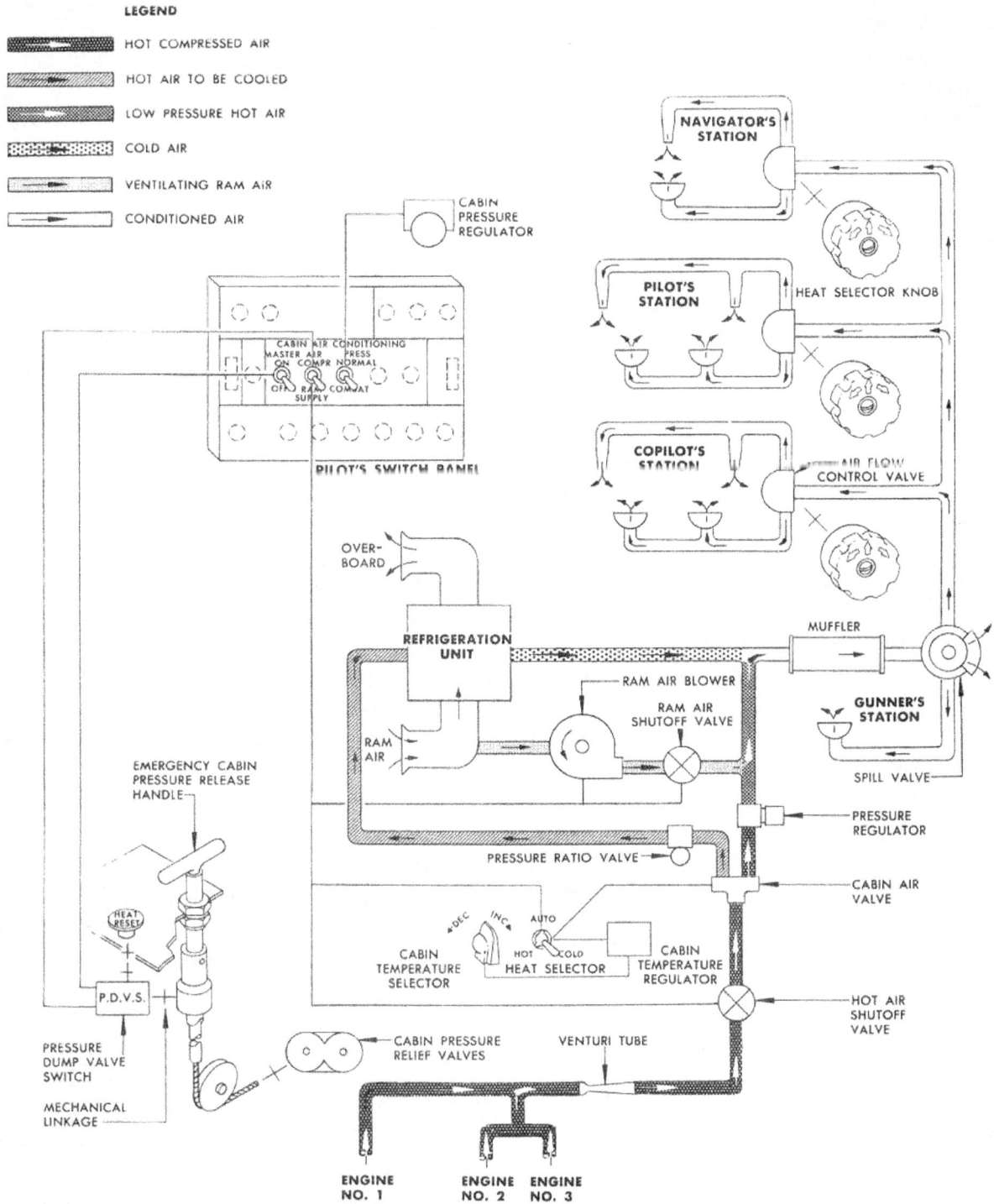

Figure 4-1. Cabin Heating, Ventilating, and Pressurizing System

b. Check to see that the cabin air selector switch is in the "COMPR" position.

c. Check to see that the pressure regulation selector switch is in the "NORMAL" position.

d. Turn the master air conditioning switch to the "ON" position. Cabin pressure is automatically controlled by the cabin pressure regulator.

NOTE

Cabin pressurizing and heating will be off whenever the master air conditioning switch is in the "OFF" position, the cabin air selector switch is in the "RAM" position, or the emergency cabin pressure release handle is pulled up. Cabin heating without pressurizing can be on only with the emergency cabin pressure release handle pulled up and the heat reset button pushed down.

4-22. EMERGENCY OPERATION.

4-23. CABIN HEATING. When either the cabin temperature selector rheostat or cabin temperature regulator fails to maintain the desired cabin temperature, actuate the heat selector switch to the "HOT" or "COLD" position to correspondingly increase or decrease the cabin temperature as required.

4-24. CABIN PRESSURIZING.

a. During combat operations, turn the cabin pressurization selector switch to the "COMBAT" position to change pressure regulator operation to provide a constant low 2.35 PSI differential pressure control above 10,500 feet.

b. In the event of cabin pressure regulator failure, pressure will be automatically relieved above 6.55 PSI differential pressure by the cabin pressure relief valves.

c. For rapid depressurization, pull the emergency cabin pressure release handle. To restore heating, if desired while depressurized, push the heat reset button.

4-24A. FOG ACCUMULATION IN THE CABIN. Under certain atmospheric conditions it is possible for fog to accumulate in the cabin while pressurized and seriously restrict visibility. If this occurs, immediately turn the cabin temperature selector rheostat to the full "INC" position (if operating under manual temperature control, hold the heat selector switch in the "HOT" position). After the cabin has cleared, reposition the cabin temperature selector rheostat (if operating under manual temperature control, actuate the heat selector switch to the "COLD" position) to obtain a cabin air temperature sufficiently higher than the original to prevent recurrence of the fog condition. If a comfortable temperature cannot be maintained without fogging, depressurize the cabin until an area with more favorable atmospheric conditions is entered.

4-25. ANTI-ICING SYSTEMS.

4-26. GENERAL.

4-27. WING ANTI-ICING. The wing, nacelle, and inboard nacelle strut leading edges are heated for anti-icing by a supply of hot air bled from the last stage of the jet engine compressors. (See figure 4-2.) Motor-driven shutoff valves, pressure regulating valves, and pressure relief valves are in each supply duct for nacelle and nacelle strut anti-icing. Engine air pressure is reduced to 5 PSI maximum for nacelle anti-icing by the pressure regulating valves. The pressure relief valves are set to relieve at 8.5 PSI in the event of failure of the pressure regulating valves. Hot air for wing anti-icing is ducted from each engine to a combination motor-actuated shutoff and pressure regulating valve assembly in each wing where the engine air pressure is reduced to 7 PSI maximum. Low pressure hot air is then ducted throughout the wing leading edge area. After passing through the leading edge ducts and double skin area, the air is exhausted overboard.

4-28. EMPENNAGE ANTI-ICING. Ram air is heated by three combustion heaters for empennage leading edge and retractable scoop anti-icing. (See figure 4-2.) The three heaters are manifolded together for maximum heating and are individually shrouded to minimize heat radiation in the heater compartment. Air under ram pressure from an intake in the dorsal serves to ventilate and pressurize, above ambient pressure, the heater compartment. Ventilating air for the shrouded heaters, fuel and electrical connections, is supplied through this same entry and is exhausted overboard through the heater exhaust shrouds. Anti-icing and heater combustion air is supplied through the retractable scoop. To prevent operation of the heaters on the ground, a pressure switch is vented to the intake duct to keep the system inoperative when intake duct pressure is less than 15 inches water pressure. A thermal switch in the intake duct also prevents heater operation when intake air temperature is above 70° F. Engine fuel is supplied through a pump, regulating valve, shutoff valve, and individual heater cycling valves for heater operation. Ignition spark is provided at the heater spark plug gap by means of ignition transformers energized from the regulated AC bus. Individual heaters, when turned on, are automatically controlled by thermal switches which cycle heater operation at 360° F. Individual heater backfire and overheat thermal switches shut off all heaters whenever any heater upstream temperature exceeds 200° F or heater downstream temperature exceeds 450° F. Fire detection thermal switches also shut off the heaters if the heater compartment temperature reaches 300° F. Individual heater no-heat indicator lights are controlled by 200° F thermal switches in the heater outlet ducts.

048073 A

4-29. WINDSHIELD ANTI-ICING. The center pane of the windshield is a bullet resistant Nesa glass window. This window is heated for anti-icing by passing high voltage unregulated alternating current across the Nesa film coating on the inside of the outer pane of glass. Unregulated alternating current of 115 volts is supplied by the engine-driven alternators and is increased to the required voltage for window heating by a transformer. Application of current to the window is controlled by an electronic bridge control system. A resistance-type temperature sensing element in the window is a part of the electronic bridge system and controls the alternating current so as to maintain a window temperature of 120° F. For preheating when the window temperature is less than 8° F, a substantially lower voltage is automatically applied to the window. In the event that the window temperature should exceed 120° F the control system will cycle at an overheat condition. A light will indicate when the window system is cycling at overheat.

4-30. CANOPY AND NOSE DEFROSTING. The nose window, windshield, and canopy are defrosted by a forced flow of cabin air directed across the inner

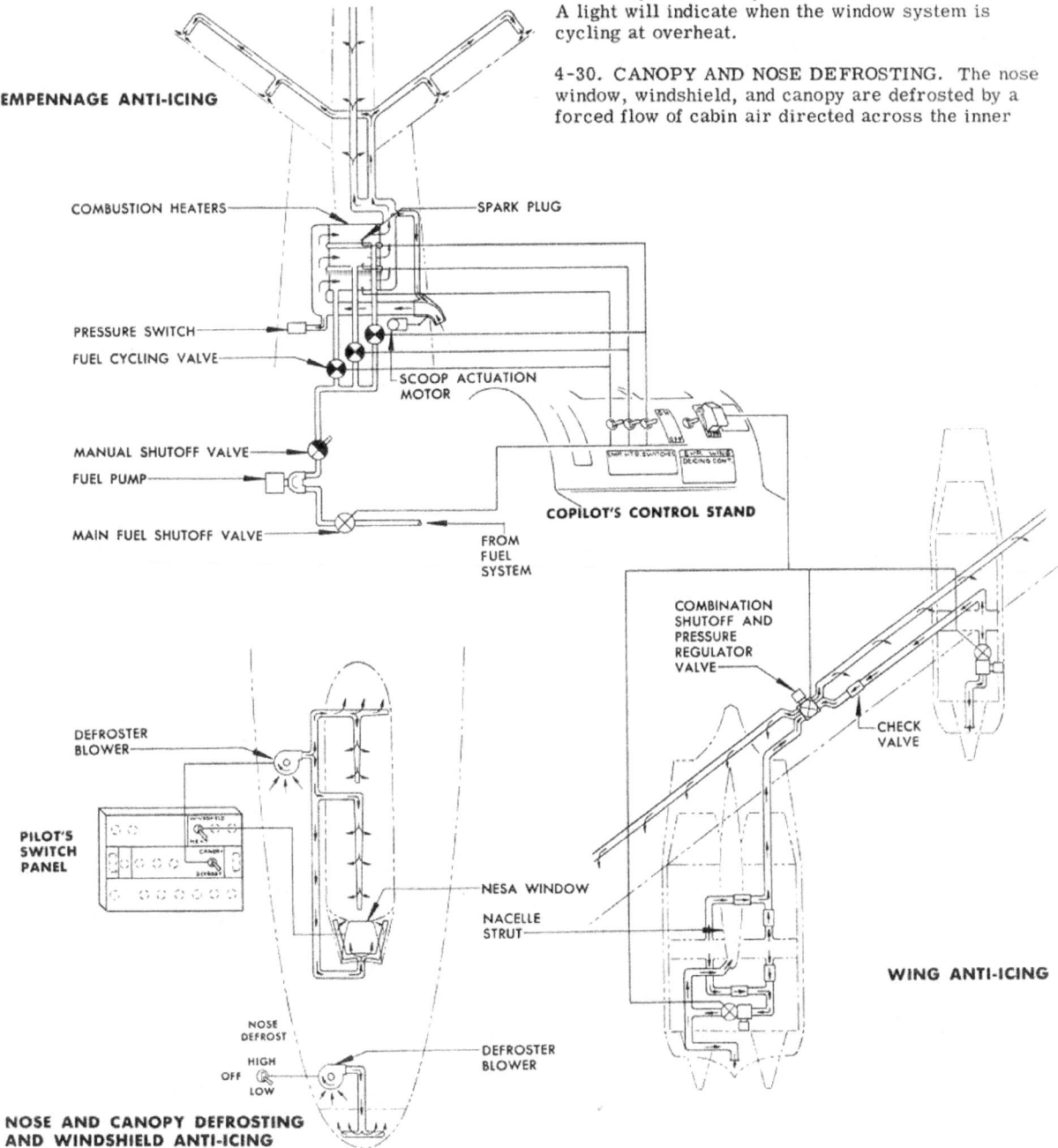

Figure 4-2. Anti-Icing Systems

surfaces by perforated ducting. (See figure 4-2.) The air flow is controlled by two-speed motor-driven blowers.

4-31. PITOT HEAT. The left and right air speed pitot tubes are heated for anti-icing by direct current heating elements contained in the pitot heads.

4-32. CONTROLS.

4-33. WING DEICING (ANTI-ICING) CONTROL SWITCH. The wing anti-icing circuit breaker type control switch (9, figure 1-15) is located on the copilot's control stand. The switch toggle is guarded to the "OFF" position. When the switch is in the "ON" position, the nacelle and wing shutoff valve motors are energized to open the valves and allow hot engine compressor air to enter the nacelle, nacelle strut, and wing leading edge areas for anti-icing. When the switch is in the "OFF" position, the nacelle and wing shutoff valve motors are energized to close the valves and shut off the flow of air to the wing and nacelle leading edge areas. An additional control circuit breaker is on the copilot's circuit breaker panel (3, figure 1-24).

4-34. EMPENNAGE DEICING (ANTI-ICING) CONTROL SWITCH. The empennage anti-icing control switch (10, figure 1-15) is on the copilot's control stand. When the switch is in the "ON" position, one no-heat indicator light for each heater will be on until the heater outlet temperature increases to 200° F, the combustion heater main fuel solenoid shutoff valve will be energized to the open position, the combustion heater fuel pump will be energized, the scoop motor will be energized to extend the scoop, and power will be supplied to the heater control circuit. When the empennage anti-icing control switch is in the "OFF" position, power will be disconnected so as to de-energize the no-heat indicator lights, the fuel pump, the heater fuel shutoff valve, the heater control circuit, and power will be supplied to operate the scoop motor to retract the scoop closing the intake air duct. The control circuit breaker is located on the copilot's circuit breaker panel (3, figure 1-24).

4-35. EMPENNAGE HEATER SWITCHES. An "ON--OFF" empennage heater switch (20, figure 1-15) for each of the three combustion heaters is on the copilot's control stand. The switches provide control of the individual combustion heaters. If the empennage anti-icing control switch is "ON," intake duct air pressure is 15 inches of water, and intake duct air temperature is less than 70° F, power will be supplied to the empennage heater switches. With power supplied and the switches in the "ON" position, the cycling fuel solenoid shutoff valves will be energized to supply fuel to the heaters and the ignition transformers will be energized by 115-volt regulated AC power to supply high voltage AC to the heater spark plugs for igniting the fuel. When the switches are in the "OFF" position, the cycling fuel solenoid shutoff valves will be de-energized to shut off the fuel supply to the heaters and the ignition transformers will be de-energized. The circuit breaker for the AC circuit is on the AC circuit breaker panel (2, figure 1-24).

4-36. WINDSHIELD HEAT SWITCH. The "ON--OFF" windshield heat circuit breaker type switch (7, figure 1-11) is on the pilot's switch panel. When the switch is in the "ON" position, DC power is supplied to the electronic control system which will automatically connect high voltage unregulated AC power to the Nesa window as required to maintain the 120° F window temperature. When the switch is in the "OFF" position, DC power is disconnected from the electronic control system which will disconnect AC power from the window. An additional DC control circuit breaker is on the copilot's circuit breaker panel (3, figure 1-24) and the unregulated AC power circuit breaker is on the AC circuit breaker panel (2, figure 1-24).

4-37. CANOPY AND NOSE DEFROST SWITCHES. The canopy defrost switch (8, figure 1-11) is on the pilot's switch panel and the nose defrost switch (17, figure 4-8) is on the bombardier's panel. These switches are marked "HIGH--OFF--LOW." When the switches are in the "HIGH" position, the defrosting blower motors are energized for high speed operation to provide maximum volume of cabin air to the nose, windshield, and canopy inner surfaces. When the switches are in the "OFF" position, the defrosting blower motors are de-energized. In the "LOW" position, the switches energize the blower motors through resistances to provide a low speed and a lower volume of cabin air to the inner nose, windshield, and canopy surfaces. The circuit breakers are on the copilot's circuit breaker panel (3, figure 1-24).

4-38. PITOT HEAT SWITCHES. Two "ON--OFF" pitot heat circuit breaker type switches (9, figure 1-11) are on the pilot's switch panel. When the switches are in the "ON" position, DC power is supplied to the heating elements in the left and right airspeed tube pitot heads for anti-icing. In the "OFF" position, the switches disconnect DC power from the heating elements. An additional control circuit breaker is on the copilot's circuit breaker panel (3, figure 1-24).

4-39. INDICATORS.

4-40. WING OVERHEAT WARNING LIGHT. A red wing overheat warning light (7, figure 1-15) is on the copilot's control stand. The light will be illuminated whenever the left or right wing leading edge area temperature, as detected by a thermal switch in each wing, exceeds 350° F. A wing overheat warning circuit test switch (8, figure 1-15) on the copilot's control stand will provide an indication of circuit continuity by the illumination of the overheat warning light when the switch is actuated to the momentary "TEST" position. In the "ON" position, the test switch reconnects the light for thermal switch operation.

4-41. EMPENNAGE HEATER NO-HEAT LIGHTS. Three amber no-heat lights (7, figure 1-15), one for each empennage combustion heater, are on the copilot's control stand. Any light will be illuminated whenever the empennage anti-icing control switch is "ON" and the corresponding heater outlet air temperature is less than 200° F.

4-41A. WINDSHIELD OVERHEAT CYCLING LIGHT.
An amber light (22, figure 1-8) on the pilot's instrument panel will illuminate when the Nesa heat system for the windshield is cycling at an overheat condition.

4-42. EMPENNAGE OVERHEAT WARNING LIGHT.
A red empennage overheat warning light (7, figure 1-15) is on the copilot's control stand. The light will be illuminated when the empennage anti-icing control switch is "ON" and any heater upstream temperature exceeds 200° F, any heater outlet temperature exceeds 450° F, or the heater compartment temperature exceeds 300° F. When the light is on, the ignition transformers, fuel cycling valves, fuel shutoff valve, and fuel pump will be de-energized, and the scoop motor will be energized to retract the ram air scoop.

NOTE

The empennage anti-icing system is electrically locked in an inoperable condition whenever the overheat warning light is on due to any heater compartment or heater overheat temperature condition.

4-43. NORMAL OPERATION.

4-44. WING ANTI-ICING. The wing anti-icing circuit breaker type control switch is guarded to the "OFF" position. The wing anti-icing system is to be operated only as required during icing conditions. Before turning the wing anti-icing control switch "ON," momentarily hold the wing overheat warning test switch in the "TEST" position and see that the warning light will operate. Release test switch, lift wing anti-icing control switch guard, and place switch in the "ON" position. During operation, reduce engine power to prevent wing overheat. To turn wing anti-icing system off, move the switch guard to actuate the control switch to the "OFF" position.

4-45. EMPENNAGE ANTI-ICING. The empennage anti-icing system is to be operated only during icing conditions.

NOTE

The pilot must establish that the nozzles installed in the empennage combustion heaters are suitable for the fuel with which the airplane has been serviced.

a. With DC power on, check for proper main regulated AC power bus voltage.
b. Turn the empennage anti-icing control switch to the "ON" position.

NOTE

The heater no-heat lights will illuminate until the combustion heaters operate and their outlet air temperature reaches 200° F.

c. Turn the empennage heater switches to the "ON" position. Use only the number of heaters required to adequately heat the empennage leading edges for anti-icing.

NOTE

The combustion heaters will not operate unless the intake duct air pressure is more than 15 inches of water and the intake duct air temperature is less than 70° F.

4-46. The individual combustion heaters will automatically shut off when the outlet air temperature increases above 360° F and restart when the outlet air temperature decreases below 360° F. To turn the empennage anti-icing system off, turn the heater switches and the empennage anti-icing control switch to their "OFF" positions.

4-47. EMERGENCY OPERATION.

4-48. EMPENNAGE ANTI-ICING. If a heater no-heat light should remain on or be illuminated after sufficient operating time has elapsed for heater outlet temperature to reach 200° F, turn the switch for the heater concerned to the "OFF" position. This should be done to shut off the supply of fuel to a heater which may be inoperative because of an ignition transformer or spark plug failure. If the empennage overheat warning light illuminates and remains illuminated, do not attempt to restart the heaters. Turn the empennage anti-icing control switch "OFF."

TABLE OF COMMUNICATIONS AND ASSOCIATED ELECTRONIC EQUIPMENT				
TYPE	DESIGNATION	USE	PRIMARY OPERATOR	FIGURE NUMBER
VHF Command	AN/ARC-3	Short range, two-way voice and code communication.	Pilot	1-13
Marker Beacon	RC-193-A	Receive location marker signals on navigation beam.	Pilot	1-8
Interphone	AAF COMBAT	Intercrew communication and use with other radio.	All crew members	1-13, 1-21 and 4-8
Radio Compass	AN/ARN-6	Reception of voice and code communication, position finding, and homing.	Pilot	1-13

Figure 4-3. Communications Equipment

048023 A

4-49. COMMUNICATIONS AND ASSOCIATED ELEC-
TRONIC EQUIPMENT.

4-50. GENERAL. The VHF command radio, marker
beacon, interphone system, and radio compass are
operated by power from the direct current power
system. In an emergency, the radio equipment can
be operated on battery power for a short period of
time.

4-51. VHF COMMAND. This equipment is turned
on or off by an "ON--OFF" switch on the pilot's
radio control panel (3, figure 1-13).

4-52. MARKER BEACON. A marker beacon light
(33, figure 1-8) is on the pilot's instrument panel.
The set is in operation whenever the direct current
power system is energized.

4-53. INTERPHONE SYSTEM. An AAF combat
interphone system with controls at all crew stations
has been provided. The interphone system is in
operation whenever the direct current power system
is energized. An interphone circuit breaker is on the
copilot's circuit breaker panel (3, figure 1-24).

4-54. RADIO COMPASS. This equipment is turned
on by an "OFF--COMP--ANT--LOOP--CONT"
switch on the pilot's radio control panel (11, figure
1-13). A compass circuit breaker is on the copilot's
circuit breaker panel (3, figure 1-24).

4-54A. LIGHTING EQUIPMENT.

LIGHTS	LOCATION	*SWITCH LOCATION
LANDING	ON FRONT OF INBOARD ENGINE NACELLES	ON PILOT'S SWITCH PANEL
POSITION	TOP OF FUSELAGE, BOTTOM OF FUSELAGE, WING TIPS, AND TAIL	POSITION LIGHTS CONTROL PANEL ON PILOT'S LEFT SIDE-WALL
PORTABLE WING ICING OBSERVATION	STOWED ON LEFT SIDE-WALL OPPOSITE CO-PILOT'S STATION	PLUGS IN SUIT HEATER RECEPTACLE

Figure 4-4. Exterior Lighting   048024 A

LIGHTS	LOCATION	*SWITCH LOCATION
PILOT' INSTRUMENT PANEL ULTRAVIOLET-FLUORESCENT	AT LEFT AND RIGHT SIDES OF PANEL	SWITCH TYPE RHEOSTAT ON LIGHT ASSEMBLY
FUEL CONTROL PANEL ULTRAVIOLET-FLUORESCENT	ON CANOPY BEAM ABOVE PANEL	SWITCH TYPE RHEOSTAT ON PANEL
FUEL CONTROL PANEL	ON LEFT AND RIGHT SIDES OF PANEL	SWITCH TYPE RHEOSTAT ON PANEL
PILOT'S SWITCH	FIRE WARNING TEST PANEL	SWITCH TYPE RHEOSTAT ON PILOT'S RADIO CONTROL PANEL
STEERING RATIO	PILOT'S INSTRUMENT PANEL ABOVE LEVER	SWITCH TYPE RHEOSTAT ON PILOT'S RADIO CONTROL PANEL
PILOT'S THROTTLE	ON CANOPY BEAM ABOVE THROTTLES	SWITCH TYPE RHEOSTAT ON PILOT'S RADIO CONTROL PANEL

LIGHTS	LOCATION	*SWITCH LOCATION
PILOT'S OXYGEN PANEL	ABOVE AND TO LEFT OF REGULATOR	SWITCH TYPE RHEOSTAT ON PILOT'S RADIO CONTROL PANEL
AUTOPILOT	ON WINDSHIELD FRAME ABOVE AUTOPILOT CONTROLS	SWITCH TYPE RHEOSTAT ON PILOT'S RADIO CONTROL PANEL
PILOT'S SPOT	RIGHT SIDE-WALL OPPOSITE PILOT'S SEAT BACK	ON LIGHT ASSEMBLY
PILOT'S FLOOD	INBOARD OF RIGHT SIDE-WALL OPPOSITE PILOT'S SEAT BACK	PILOT'S RADIO CONTROL PANEL
COPILOT'S INSTRUMENT PANEL ULTRAVIOLET-FLUORESCENT	AT LEFT AND RIGHT SIDES OF PANEL	SWITCH TYPE RHEOSTAT ON LIGHT ASSEMBLY

*All lighting circuit breakers are on the copilot's circuit breaker panel (3, figure 1-25).
Figure 4-5 (Sheet 1 of 2 Sheets). Interior Lighting   048025aA

LIGHTS	LOCATION	*SWITCH LOCATION	LIGHTS	LOCATION	*SWITCH LOCATION
COPILOT'S CIR-CUIT BREAKER PANEL	COPILOT'S SIDEWALL ABOVE PANEL	SWITCH TYPE RHEOSTAT ON COPILOT'S SIDEWALL	NAVIGATOR'S TABLE	ON SIDEWALL ABOVE TABLE	SWITCH TYPE RHEOSTAT ON BOMBARDIER'S PANEL
COPILOT'S CIR-CUIT BREAKER PANEL	COPILOT'S INTERPHONE CONTROL PANEL	SWITCH TYPE RHEOSTAT ON COPILOT'S SIDEWALL	BOMBARDIER'S SPOT	ON HATCH FRAME ABOVE BOM-BARDIER'S PANEL	SWITCH TYPE RHEOSTAT ON BOMBARDIER'S PANEL
AC CIRCUIT BREAKER PANEL	ON CANOPY BEAM ABOVE PANEL	SWITCH TYPE RHEOSTAT ON COPILOT'S SIDEWALL	NAVIGATOR'S DOME	ON RIGHT HATCH BEAM ABOVE NAVI-GATOR'S SEAT	ON BOMBARD-IER'S PANEL
HYDRAULIC CONTROL PANEL	ON COPILOT'S SIDEWALL FORWARD OF PANEL	SWITCH TYPE RHEOSTAT ON COPILOT'S SIDEWALL	ENTRANCE	ABOVE EN-TRANCE DOOR IN PASSAGE	JUST INSIDE EN-TRANCE DOOR
COPILOT'S OXYGEN PANEL	ABOVE AND TO LEFT OF REGULATOR	SWITCH TYPE RHEOSTAT ON COPILOT'S SIDEWALL	WALKWAY DOME	UNDERSIDE OF CANOPY BEAM ALONG WALKWAY	JUST INSIDE EN-TRANCE DOOR, IN PILOT'S AND COPILOT'S OXY-GEN PANELS, AND ON BOM-BARDIER'S PANEL
COPILOT'S SPOT	ON COPILOT'S CONTROL STAND	ON LIGHT AS-SEMBLY			
COPILOT'S FLOOR	INBOARD OF RIGHT SIDE-WALL OPPO-SITE PILOT'S SEAT BACK	ON COPILOT'S SIDEWALL	PASSAGE DOME	IN PASSAGE ABOVE DOOR TO CRAWL-WAY	ON LEFT IN PASSAGE AFT OF ENTRANCE DOOR
GUNNER'S PANEL	AT TOP OF PANEL	SWITCH TYPE RHEOSTAT AT TOP OF PANEL	CRAWLWAY DOME	IN CRAWL-WAY CEILING	ON LEFT IN PASSAGE AFT OF ENTRANCE DOOR
GUNNER'S SPOT	BELOW GUNNER'S PANEL	ON LIGHT AS-SEMBLY	BOMB BAY WORK	ON BOMB BAY FOR-WARD BULK-HEAD	ON CEILING IN FORWARD END OF BOMB BAY
NAVIGATOR'S INSTRUMENT ULTRAVIOLET-FLUORESCENT	AT RIGHT OF PANEL	SWITCH TYPE RHEOSTAT ON LIGHT ASSEM-BLY	BOMB BAY FLOOD	ON CEILING IN BOMB BAY	ON CEILING IN FORWARD END OF BOMB BAY
BOMBARDIER'S PANEL	AT TOP OF PANEL	SWITCH TYPE RHEOSTAT AT BOTTOM OF PANEL	BOMB BAY DOME	ON CEILING IN BOMB BAY	ON CEILING IN FORWARD END OF BOMB BAY

*All lighting circuit breakers are on the copilot's
circuit breaker panel (3, figure 1-25).

Figure 4-5 (Sheet 2 of 2 Sheets). Interior Lighting

G48025b

CREW MEMBER OXYGEN DURATION IN HOURS

CABIN ALTITUDE FEET	GAGE PRESSURE — PSI							BELOW 100
	400	350	300	250	200	150	100	
40,000	4.7	4.0	3.4	2.7	2.0	1.3	0.7	EMERGENCY DESCEND TO ALTITUDE NOT REQUIRING OXYGEN
	4.7	4.0	3.4	2.7	2.0	1.3	0.7	
35,000	4.7	4.0	3.4	2.7	2.0	1.3	0.7	
	4.7	4.0	3.4	2.7	2.0	1.3	0.7	
30,000	3.5	3.0	2.5	2.0	1.5	1.0	0.5	
	3.5	3.0	2.5	2.0	1.5	1.0	0.5	
25,000	2.8	2.4	2.0	1.6	1.2	0.8	0.4	
	3.3	2.8	2.4	1.9	1.4	0.9	0.5	
20,000	2.3	1.9	1.6	1.3	1.0	0.6	0.3	
	3.7	3.2	2.7	2.1	1.6	1.1	0.5	
15,000	1.8	1.5	1.3	1.0	0.8	0.5	0.3	
	4.5	3.9	3.2	2.6	1.9	1.3	0.6	
10,000	1.5	1.3	1.1	0.9	0.7	0.4	0.2	
	6.0	5.2	4.3	3.4	2.6	1.7	0.9	

BLACK FIGURES INDICATE DILUTER LEVER "NORMAL"

RED FIGURES INDICATE DILUTER LEVER "100%"

CYLINDERS: 10 TYPE D-2
CREW: 3

Figure 4-6. Oxygen Duration

4-55. OXYGEN SYSTEM.

4-56. GENERAL.

4-57. A low pressure oxygen system supplied by 10 Type D-2 oxygen cylinders, is installed in the airplane. The cylinders are located beneath the cockpit floor inside, and on the lower right side, of the pressurized compartment shell. For combat safety, each oxygen station is supplied from two distribution lines through automatic check valves. The complete oxygen system may be serviced through a single filler valve located in a service hatch on the right side of the fuselage forward of the wing. Two portable oxygen units and recharging facilities are provided. One unit is located on the lower forward side of the navigator's station and one on the cockpit left side wall. A pressure breathing demand type oxygen mask will be used by each crew member.

4-58. CONTROLS.

4-59. PRESSURE REGULATOR DILUTER LEVER. A "NORMAL OXYGEN--100% OXYGEN" dilutor lever is provided on each regulator to select a normal automatic mixture of air and oxygen or to select 100% oxygen for emergency use.

4-60. PRESSURE DIAL. A pressure dial is installed on each regulator which provides safety pressure in the oxygen mask above 30,000 feet and pressure breathing above 40,000 feet.

4-61. INDICATORS.

4-62. PRESSURE GAGES. Each crew station is provided an oxygen pressure gage. In addition, the copilot is provided a pressure gage at his gunnery station.

048026 A

4-63. FLOW INDICATORS. Each crew station and the copilot's gunnery station are also provided an oxygen flow indicator.

4-64. NORMAL OPERATION.

4-65. The regulator dilutor lever should always be set at the "NORMAL OXYGEN" position except under emergency conditions (see paragraph 4-66). The dial of the oxygen regulator should be set as follows:
 a. For cabin altitudes below 30,000 feet, leave the dial at the "NORMAL" position.
 b. For cabin altitudes between 30,000 feet and 40,000 feet, set dial at the "SAFETY" position.
 c. For cabin altitudes above 40,000 feet, set the dial to the corresponding altitude.

4-66. EMERGENCY OPERATION.

4-67. With symptoms of anoxia or if smoke or fumes should enter the cabin, immediately put on oxygen masks and set the regulator dilutor lever to "100% OXYGEN."

CAUTION

When dilutor lever is positioned to "100% OXYGEN," the pilot will immediately be informed of this action as the use of "100% OXYGEN" will reduce oxygen duration of the airplane.

4-68. In the event of accidental loss of cabin pressure, immediately turn the pressure dial of the oxygen regulator to "ABOVE 45M" position and tighten mask to hold pressure. After the emergency is over, reset the pressure dial.

4-69. If the oxygen regulator should become inoperative, disconnect mask from the airplane oxygen system and connect it to a portable oxygen unit. If an adequately filled portable unit is not available, pull the cord of the H-2 emergency oxygen cylinder.

WARNING

When use of H-2 emergency oxygen cylinder becomes necessary, the pilot will be informed of this action so that he can immediately descend to an altitude at which oxygen is not required.

4-70. NAVIGATOR'S EQUIPMENT.

4-71. Because these airplanes are designated as "Service Test" airplanes, varying configurations of operational equipment may be expected by the flight crew. On all airplanes, a one-man navigator-bombardier-radar operator's station is installed in the nose. Equipment essential to the function of this crew member is installed for his convenient operation. The navigator's seat is centrally located and rotatable to the right with navigation, bombing, and radar equipment adjacent.

4-72. A horizontal bombsight and bombsight stabilizer are installed in the nose of the compartment, flanked by a radar indicator, the bombardier's instrument panel, and bombing control units. A navigator's table is located to the right of the navigator's seat. The following units, or space and structural provisions for the units, are installed on some airplanes: radar control box, navigation unit, oxygen regulator, table lamp, ballistics unit, interphone panel, heated suit control, bombardier's control panel including indicator lights and switches, and stowage space for a navigator's kit.

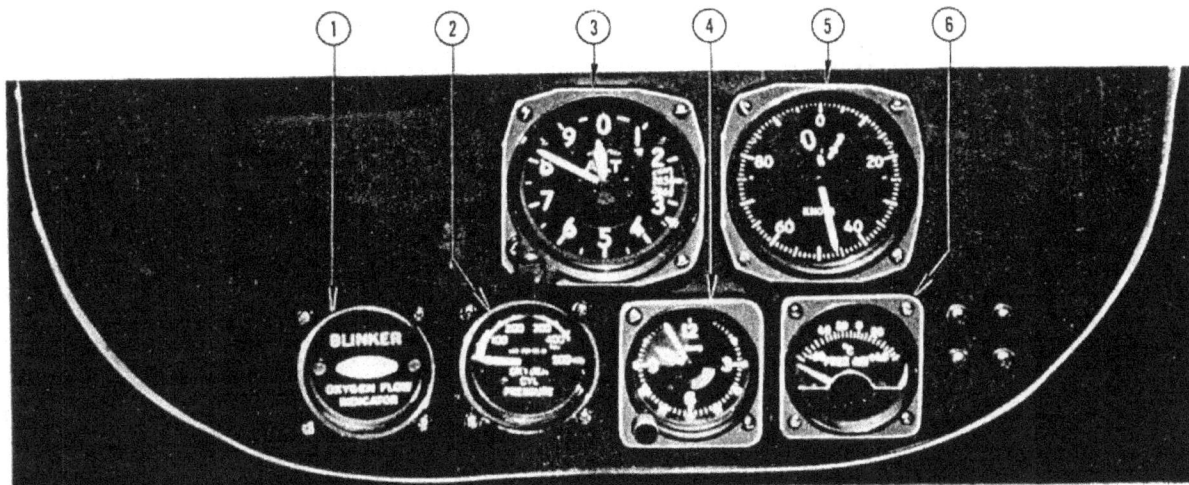

LEGEND
1. OXYGEN FLOW INDICATOR
2. OXYGEN PRESSURE INDICATOR
3. ALTIMETER
4. CLOCK
5. AIRSPEED INDICATOR
6. FREE AIR TEMPERATURE INDICATOR

Figure 4-7. Navigator's Instrument Panel

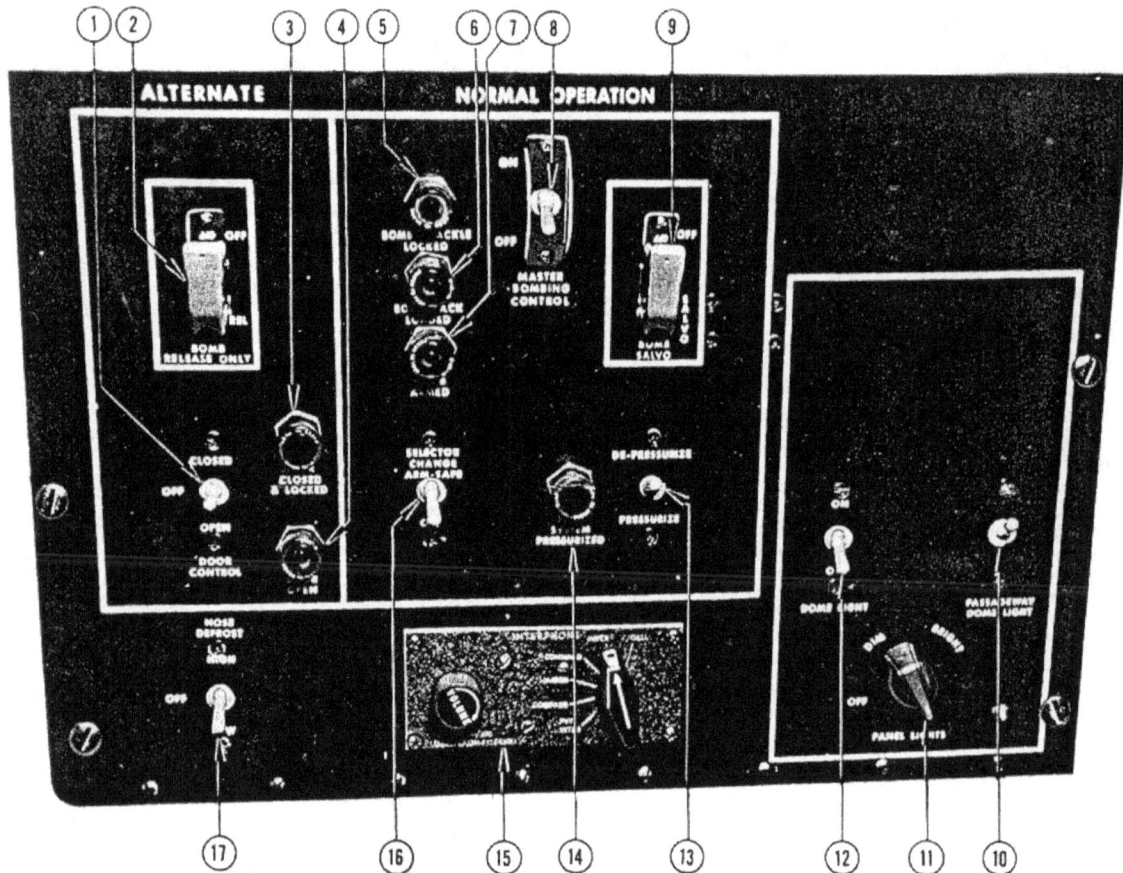

LEGEND

1. BOMB DOOR CONTROL SWITCH
2. BOMB RELEASE SWITCH
3. BOMB DOOR LIGHT
4. BOMB DOOR LIGHT
5. BOMB SHACKLE LIGHT
6. BOMB SHACKLE LIGHT
7. BOMB ARMED LIGHT
8. MASTER BOMBING CONTROL SWITCH
9. BOMB SALVE SWITCH
10. PASSAGEWAY (WALKWAY) DOME LIGHT SWITCH
11. PANEL LIGHT RHEOSTAT
12. DOME LIGHT SWITCH
13. MAIN (HYDRAULIC) SYSTEM CHARGING VALVE SWITCH
14. MAIN (HYDRAULIC) SYSTEM PRESSURE LIGHT
15. INTERPHONE CONTROL PANEL
16. BOMB ARMING SWITCH
17. NOSE DEFROSTER SWITCH

Figure 4-8. Bombardier's Panel

4-73. BOMBING EQUIPMENT.

4-74. A single purpose bomb bay is provided which will accommodate a 10,000 pound bomb. Space and structural provisions are made for 1000, 2000, 4000, 12,000, and 22,000 pound general purpose bombs and racks. On some airplanes a Type K-2 radar bombing, navigational, and computing system is installed. The bomb bay doors are hydraulically operated by pressure from either the main or emergency hydraulic system. The doors are controlled by door control switches (30, figure 1-8 and 1, figure 4-8), by bomb salvo switches (23, figure 1-8 and 9, figure 4-8), or by the bombing system.

4-75. PHOTOGRAPHIC EQUIPMENT.

4-76. Space and structural provisions are made for the addition of a Type A-8, A-11A, A-17A, or A-27A aerial camera. Provisions are also made for the addition of a photographic electrical system, photographic vacuum system, camera heating system, intervalometer, and the navigator's photographic equipment controls.

4-77. GUNNERY EQUIPMENT.

4-78. The copilot is provided a gunnery station (figure 1-16), aft of his normal station, which he can use by rotating his seat. This station includes a table, oxygen equipment, and space and structural provisions for the addition of electronic sighting and control equipment for a tail turret.

4-79. Space and structural provisions are made for the addition of an uninhabited tail turret mounting two type M-3, caliber .50 machine guns.

04804?

APPENDIX ▮ OPERATING DATA

PRESSURE ALTITUDE FEET	CALIBRATED AIR SPEED – KNOTS								CORRECTION AND V_{max}	
	100	150	200	250	300	350	400	450		V_{max}
S. L.	- - -	- - -	- - -	- - -	- - -	- - -	- - -	- - -	- - -	456
5,000	- - -	- - -	- - -	.5	1.5	2.5	3.5	4.5	5.0	456
10,000	- - -	.5	1.0	1.5	3.0	4.5	6.5	9.0	9.5	456
15,000	- - -	1.0	1.5	3.0	5.0	7.5	11.5	- - -	14.5	436
20,000	.5	1.5	3.0	5.0	8.0	12.5	11.0		17.0	400
25,000	.5	2.0	4.0	7.0	11.5	17.0	- - -	- - -	18.0	363
30,000	.5	2.5	5.0	9.5	15.0	- - -	- - -	- - -	18.5	328
35,000	1.0	3.0	6.5	12.0	- - -	- - -	- - -	- - -	18.0	292
40,000	1.0	4.0	8.0	15.5	- - -	- - -	- - -	- - -	15.5	250

COMPRESSIBILITY CORRECTION TABLE
CALIBRATED AIR SPEED – CORRECTION = EQUIVALENT AIR SPEED

NOTE: Because position error is zero on this airplane, IAS = CAS and no correction table is needed to obtain CAS.

DATA: From mach vs. calibrated air speed vs. pressure altitude plot
DATA BASIS: Calculated
DATE: 1 July 1950
REMARKS: Table applies only to NACA standard day
V_{max}: From Calculated Data

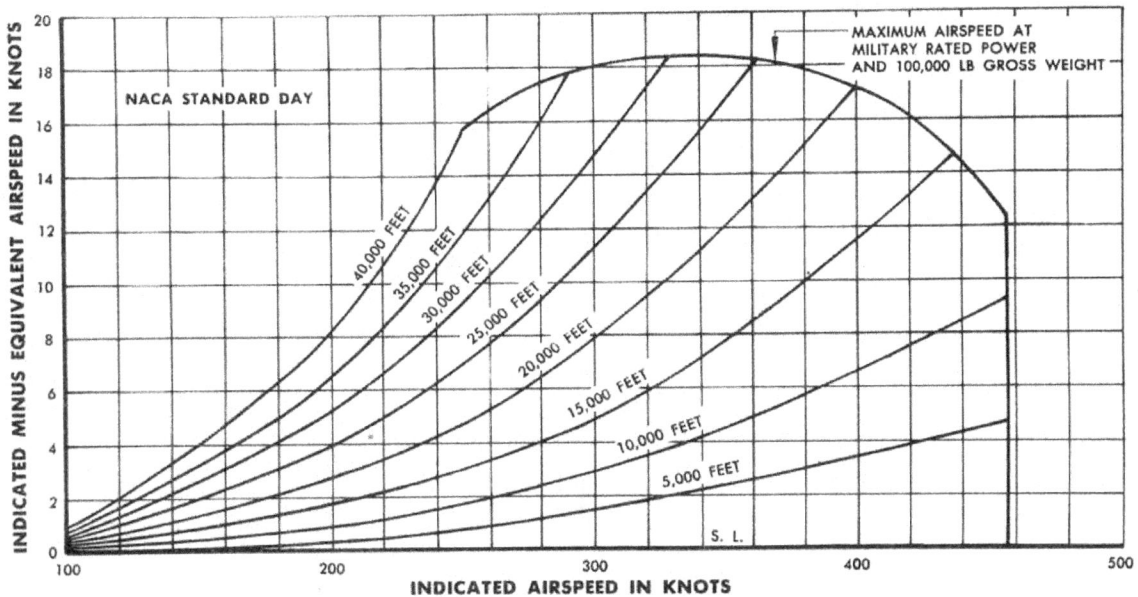

Figure A-1. Compressibility Correction

EXHAUST TEMPERATURE

	100° C	Minimum for flight
	260° C to 655° C	Continuous Operation
	690° C	Maximum for flight
	870° C	Maximum during starting and acceleration only

OIL PRESSURE

	2 PSI	Minimum for flight
	5 PSI to 25 PSI	Continuous operation
	30 PSI	Maximum

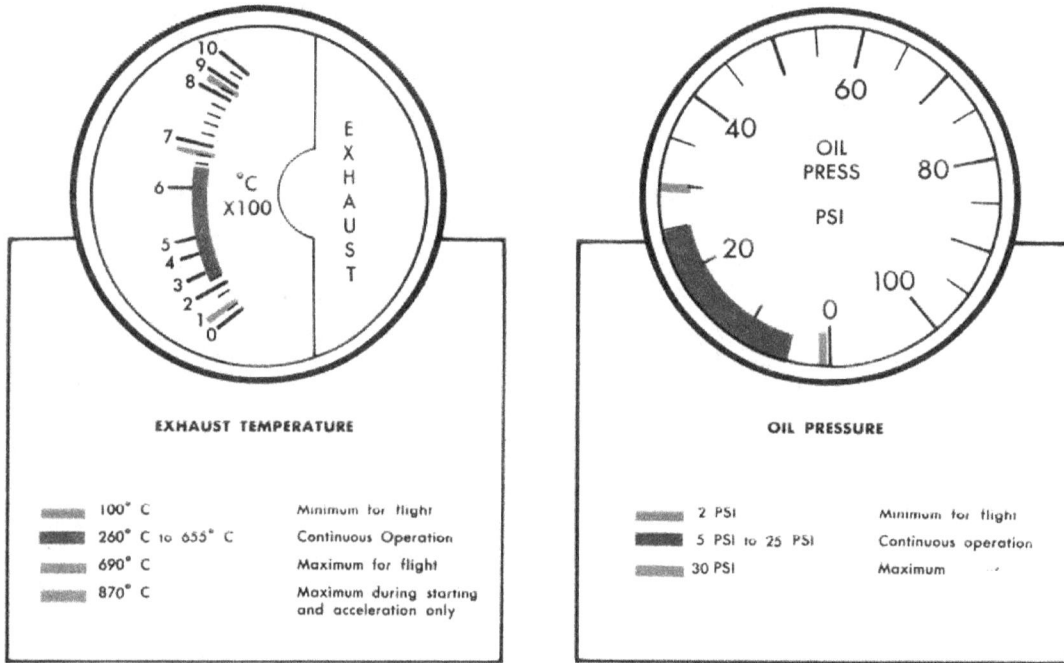

ENGINE LIMITS APPLICABLE TO ALL FUEL GRADES

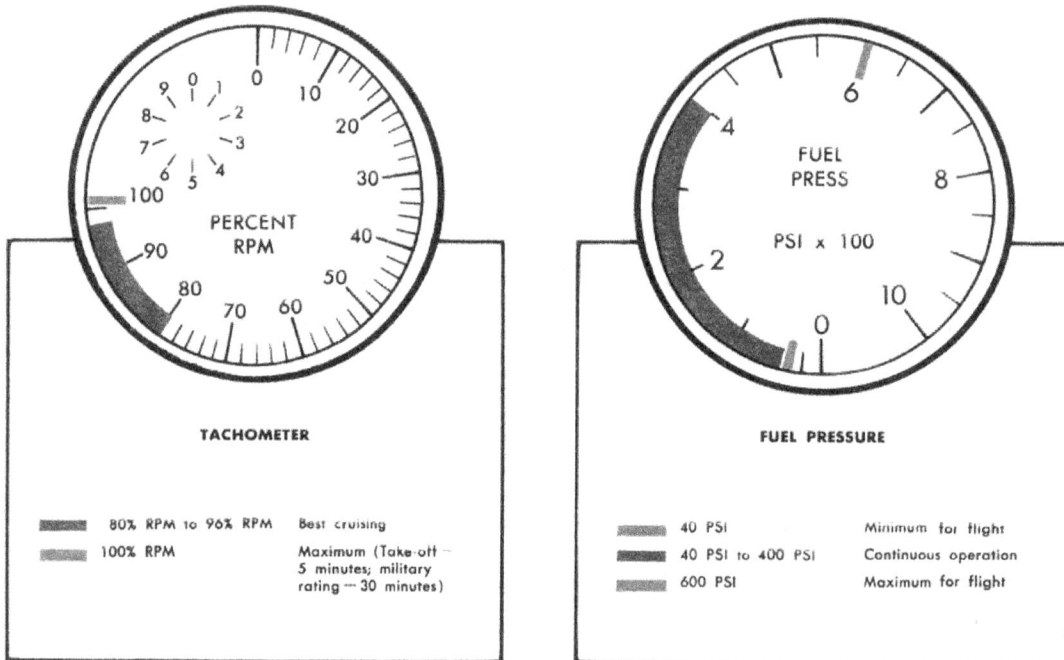

TACHOMETER

	80% RPM to 96% RPM	Best cruising
	100% RPM	Maximum (Take-off — 5 minutes; military rating — 30 minutes)

FUEL PRESSURE

	40 PSI	Minimum for flight
	40 PSI to 400 PSI	Continuous operation
	600 PSI	Maximum for flight

Figure A-2 (Sheet 1 of 3 Sheets). Instrument Markings

048029aA

MAXIMUM ALLOWABLE AIRSPEED

▬▬▬ 180 KNOTS   Full flaps (Landing gear extending 305 KNOTS)

The instrument setting is such that the red pointer will move to
indicate the limiting structural airspeed of 456 knots or the airspeed
representing the limiting Mach Number of .85, whichever is less.

ACCELEROMETER

▬▬▬ 2 g   Maximum at maximum gross weight
▬▬▬ 3 g   Maximum at design gross weight

MACHMETER

▬▬▬ .85   Maximum

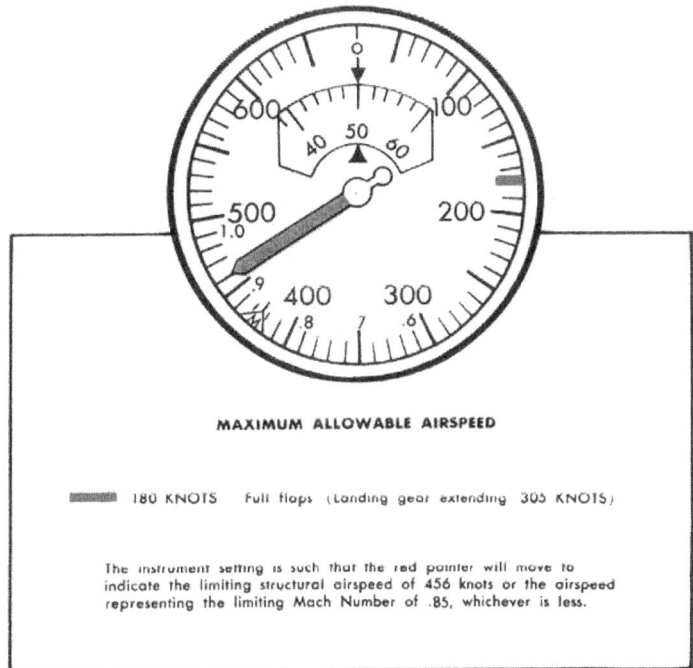

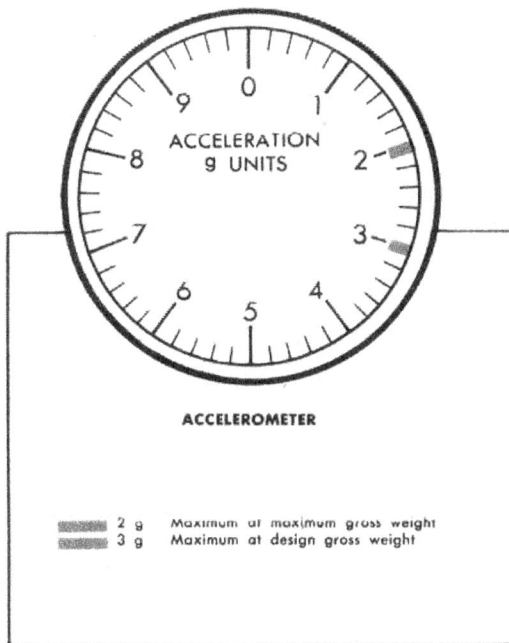

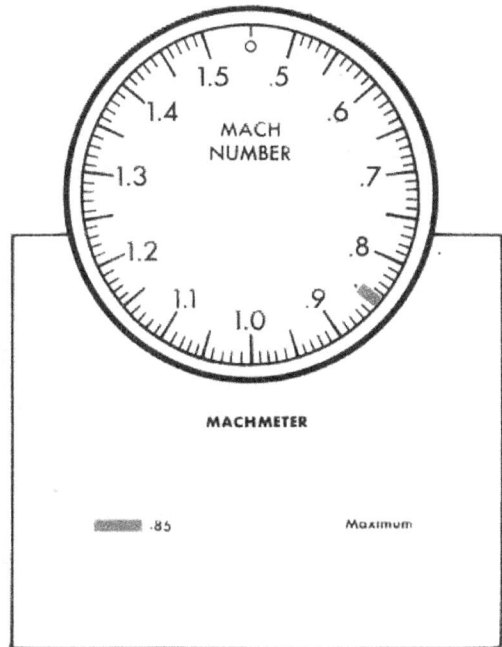

Figure A-2 (Sheet 2 of 3 Sheets). Instrument Markings

0480296A

MAIN SYSTEM HYDRAULIC PRESSURE

	2000 PSI	Minimum
	2500 PSI to 3000 PSI	Normal
	3450 PSI	Maximum

EMERGENCY SYSTEM HYDRAULIC PRESSURE

	1500 PSI	Minimum
	2500 PSI to 3100 PSI	Normal
	3450 PSI	Maximum

WARNING
Pressures below 1500 PSI are accumulator air preload pressure; below 1500 PSI the emergency system hydraulic pressure will be zero

MAIN BRAKE SYSTEM HYDRAULIC PRESSURE

	1500 PSI	Minimum
	2000 PSI to 3000 PSI	Normal
	3450 PSI	Maximum

WARNING
Pressures below 1500 PSI are accumulator air preload pressure; below 1500 PSI the main brake system hydraulic pressure will be zero

EMERGENCY BRAKE SYSTEM HYDRAULIC PRESSURE

	1000 PSI	Minimum
	1700 PSI	One brake application remaining
	1700 PSI to 3000 PSI	Normal
	3450 PSI	Maximum

WARNING
Pressures below 1000 PSI are accumulator air preload pressure; below 1000 PSI the emergency brake system hydraulic pressure will be zero

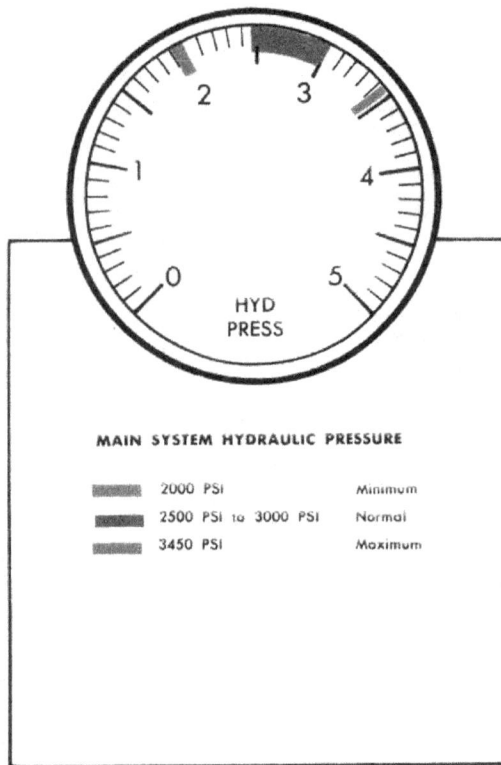

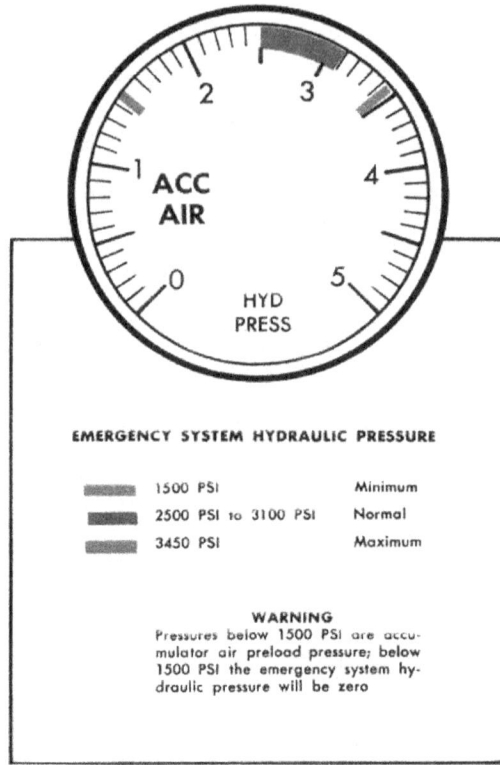

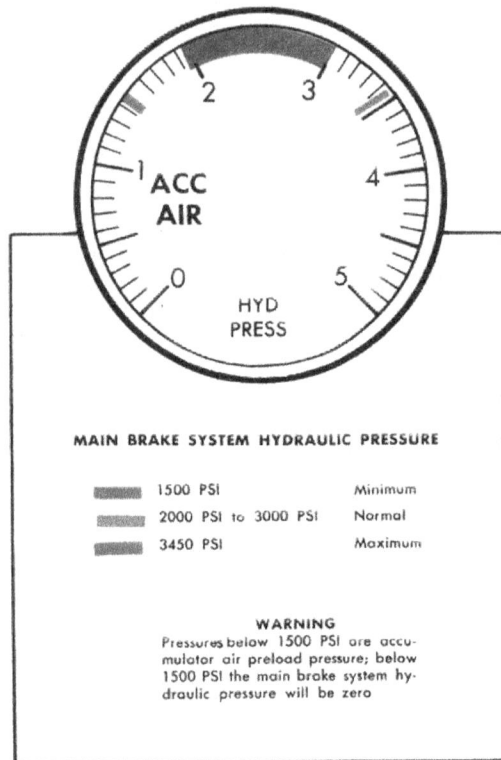

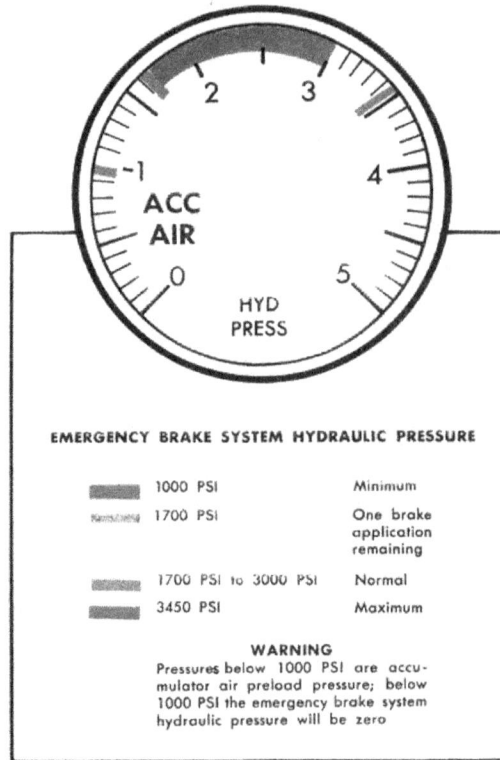

Figure A-2 (Sheet 3 of 3 Sheets). Instrument Markings

048029 A

Revised 30 October 1950

PRESSURE ALTITUDE IN FEET

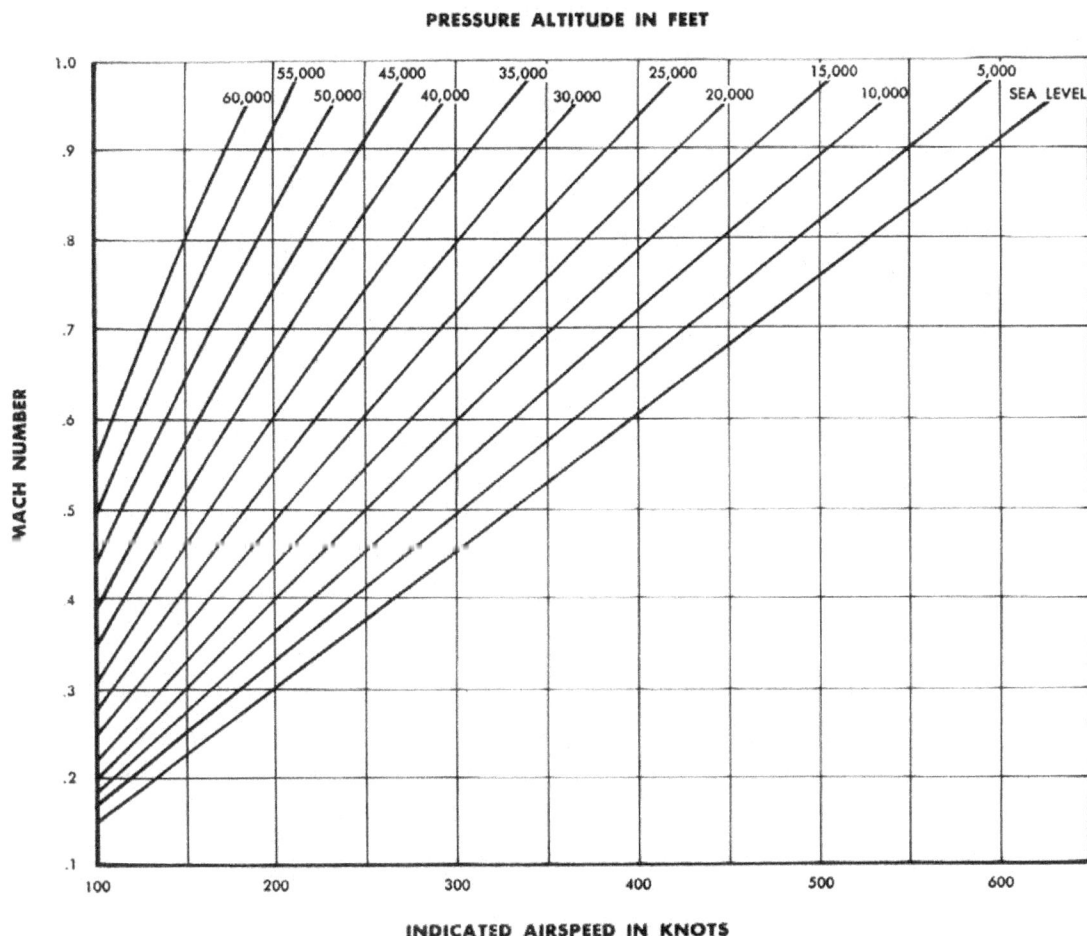

Figure A-3. Mach Number Conversion

A-1. EXHAUST GAS TEMPERATURE CORRECTION.

A-2. To obtain the correct exhaust gas temperature for 100% RPM take-offs, the nozzle area must be corrected by the installation or removal of area reducing tabs. To arrive at the correct area, accomplish the following calculations:
a. From figure A-4 find the "Desired Stabilized Exhaust Gas Temperature" corresponding to the anticipated outside air temperature at take-off. For example, the "Desired Stabilized Exhaust Gas Temperature" for a 30° C day is 683° C.
b. Transferring this value to figure A-5, find the intersection of the "Desired Stabilized Exhaust Gas Temperature" line with the "Actual Stabilized Exhaust Gas Temperature" line assumed to be 650° C for this problem (obtained on engine run-up). Proceed up the applicable line to find the required

"Nozzle Area Decrease (or Increase)"; this is the tab change that should be made; in this case a nozzle area decrease of 5 square inches requiring the installation of two 2.7 square inch tabs.

A-3. THRUST CALCULATION.

A-4. From figure A-6 it is possible to compute the percent of standard rated sea level thrust that is available, by the following method:
a. Follow the "Stabilized Exhaust Gas Temperature" line until it intersects the appropriate "Outside Air Temperature" line.
b. Drop down to the appropriate "Pressure Altitude" line, assumed to be 4000 feet for this problem.
c. Proceed over to the "Thrust Available" scale; in this case the "Thrust Available" will be 82.5% of the standard sea level rated thrust of 5,420 pounds or 4,580 pounds.

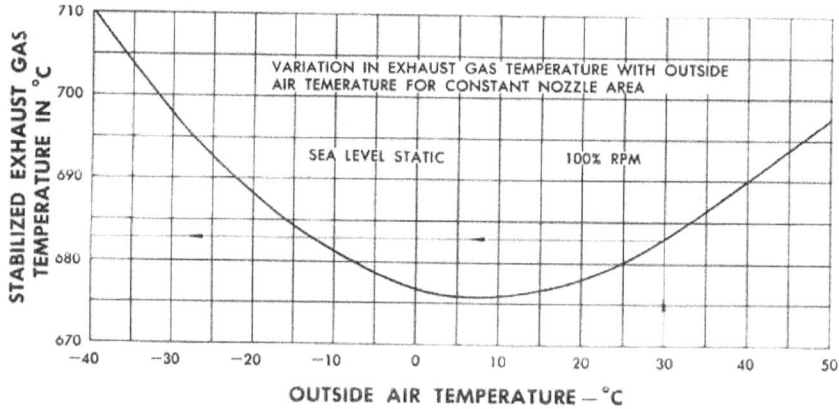

Figure A-4. Exhaust Gas Temperature Correction

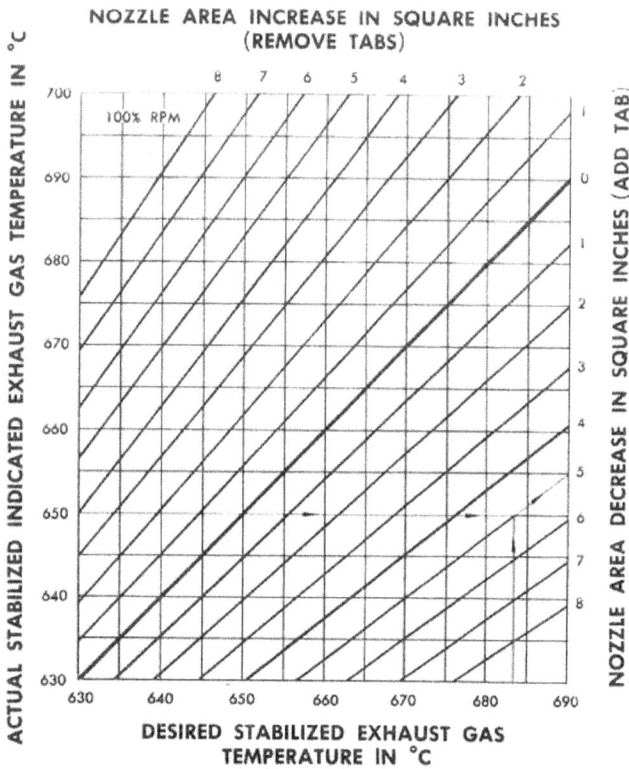

Figure A-5. Exhaust Gas Temperature Nozzle Area
Correction

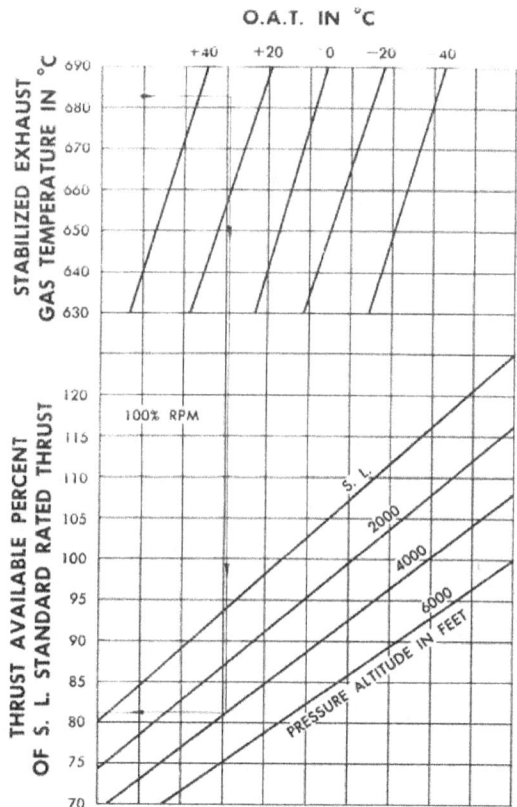

Figure A-6. Static Thrust Correction

WARSHIPS DVD SERIES

WARSHIPS: PEARL HARBOR TO MIDWAY

PEARL HARBOR TO MIDWAY

THE AIRCRAFT CARRIER WAR

1941-1942

WARSHIPS DVD VOL. 4

DVD VIDEO

HISTORIC U.S. NAVY FILMS
ON DVD!

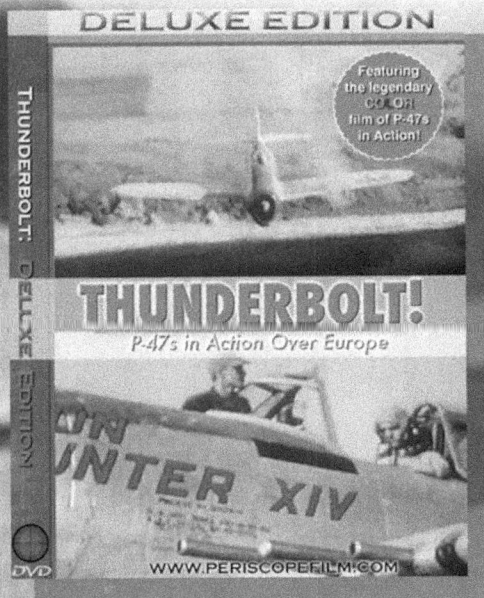

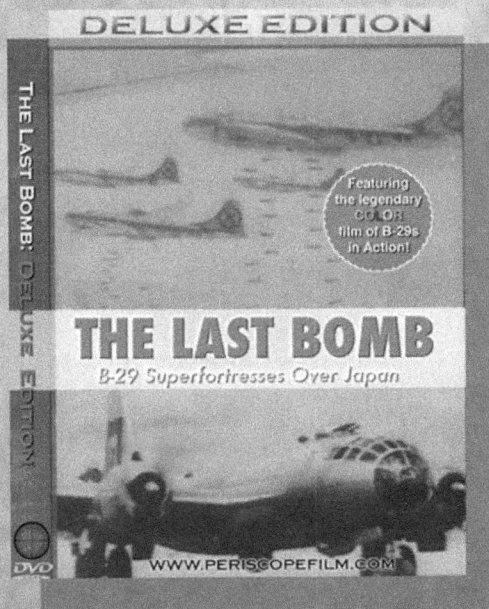

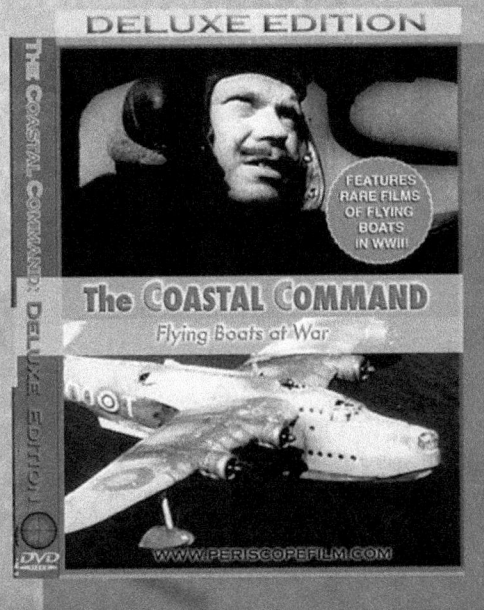

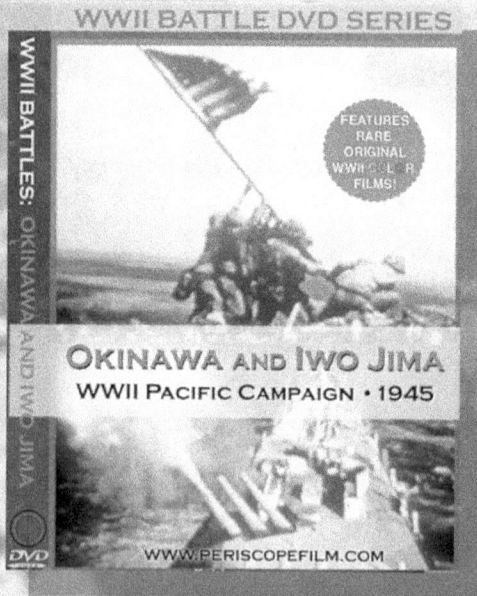

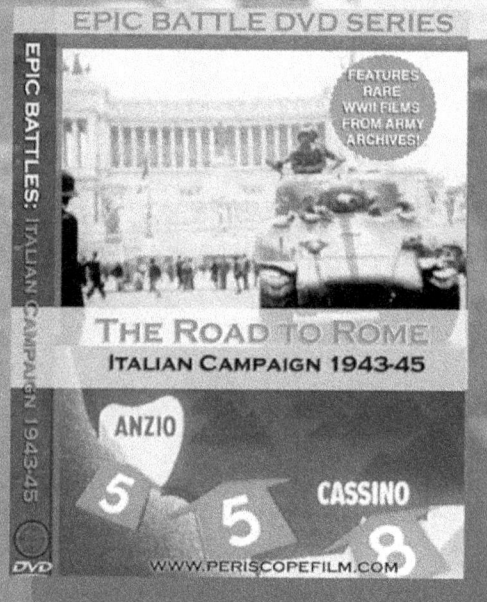

www.ingramcontent.com/pod-product-compliance
Lightning Source LLC
Chambersburg PA
CBHW080535090426
42733CB00015B/2589